DYSLEXIA

ACTION PLAN LEARNING

Glynis Hannell

David Fulton Publishers Ltd
The Chiswick Centre, 414 Chiswick High Road, London W4 5TF

www.fultonpublishers.co.uk

First published in Australia in 2003 by Palmer Educational Publications,
21 Palmer Lane, North Adelaide, South Australia 5006
First published in Great Britain by David Fulton Publishers 2004

David Fulton Publishers is a division of Granada Learning Limited, part of ITV plc.

Note: The right of Glynis Hannell to be identified as the author of this work has been asserted by her in accordance with the Copyright, Designs and Patents Act 1988.

British Library Cataloguing in Publication Data
A catalogue record for this book is available from the British Library.

ISBN 1–84312–214–6

Printed and bound in Spain

CHAPTER 4: WRITING AND SPELLING

CHAPTER 5: MATHEMATICS

CHAPTER 6: MEMORY

CHAPTER 7: CONCENTRATION

CHAPTER 8: MOTIVATION

CHAPTER 9: PARENTS, PROFESSIONALS AND HELPERS

APPENDIX

chapter 1
INTRODUCTION TO DYSLEXIA

WHAT IS DYSLEXIA?

There is no simple answer to the question 'What is dyslexia?' because it is a complex condition that varies widely from one individual to another. All dyslexic students will experience some difficulties with reading, spelling, writing and possibly mathematics. Some may have more difficulty with spelling, others may find their greatest challenge in fluent reading or getting their ideas on paper, each individual is different.

Under achievement is one of the hallmarks of a dyslexic student. Difficulties in the basic skills of reading, writing and perhaps mathematics are the almost inevitable consequences of dyslexia. Whilst not all students with learning difficulties have dyslexia, virtually all dyslexic students will have problems with learning in school. Although under achievement cannot by itself be used to diagnose dyslexia, it is often one of the clearest indicators that the student may have a learning disorder such as dyslexia. Under achievement means that a student is not performing to the level that we might reasonably expect when their age, ability and education is taken into consideration.

Dyslexic students can often be recognised by the level of their responsiveness to intervention. Whilst we can expect all students to respond to appropriate intervention, we know that in comparison to fellow students without dyslexia, dyslexic students need more intervention for a longer period of time to make the same degree of progress.

Inconsistent performance is another hallmark of the dyslexic student. Work which they can do quite well one day seems to be too difficult the next.

The following is a definition of dyslexia as adopted by the Research Committee of the International Dyslexia Association in August 2002

Dyslexia is a specific learning disability that is neurobiological in origin. It is characterised by difficulties with accurate and/or fluent word recognition and by poor spelling and decoding abilities. These difficulties typically result from a deficit in the phonological component of language that is often unexpected in relation to other cognitive abilities and the provision of effective classroom instruction. Secondary consequences may include problems in reading comprehension and reduced reading experience that can impede growth of vocabulary and background knowledge.

Dyslexia is also sometimes referred to as a:
> *Learning disability*
> *Specific learning difficulty*
> *Reading disorder*

PREVALENCE

The British Dyslexia Association states that around 4% of the population is severely dyslexic and a further 6% have mild to moderate problems.

Statistically, there are likely to be between one and three students with dyslexia in any class of thirty students. This of course will vary from year to year, depending on the distribution of students to each class, some years there will be four, five or even more dyslexic students in one class. Because it is such a common condition it is unusual for a class to have no dyslexic students.

Dyslexia occurs across all ethnic groups and in all socio-economic classes. It also occurs in all languages, although the particular pattern of difficulties tends to vary between languages. It is a lifelong condition, although with appropriate intervention the effects of the difficulty may be reduced over the long term.

Although some dyslexics have ongoing, severe problems with literacy for their whole lifespan, many dyslexics proceed to further study, including higher education.

ASSOCIATED CONDITIONS

Dyslexia and Attention Deficit Disorder frequently occur together, although the link between the two conditions is not, as yet, fully understood. Approximately 30% of dyslexic students have Attention Deficit Disorder. Low self-confidence, anxiety and motivational difficulties can be consequences of the difficulties experienced in acquiring basic literacy skills. In some cases behavioural problems may follow.

By chance a dyslexic student may also have other difficulties or disabilities that are not in any way connected with dyslexia.

There are other types of specific learning difficulties as well as dyslexia. Students may have more than one type of learning disorder.

Specific arithmetic/mathematical disorder

This is learning disability in which the student has particular, severe problems in understanding mathematical concepts and/or performing calculations. It can occur independently of dyslexia, but it is often part and parcel of the dyslexic disorder.

Dysgraphia or specific writing disorder

Dysgraphia is a writing difficulty caused by a neurological processing problem (often Developmental Coordination Disorder, or Dyspraxia). It is not due to poor muscle strength, but is caused by irregularities in the neural pathways that manage the link between brain and hand. A student with dysgraphia finds it difficult to form letters and may have particular problems with sustained writing e.g they may be able to write neatly for a few words, but then their control deteriorates sharply, and their writing becomes increasingly messy. Although appropriate treatment and practice is appropriate, it will not necessarily 'cure' the problem.

INTELLECTUALLY GIFTED DYSLEXIC STUDENTS

Intellectually gifted students with dyslexia are an important group, whose needs do need to be addressed. These youngsters may well be performing within the average range for their age group but significantly under achieving when their intelligence is taken into consideration. The level of frustration for these students is often extremely high and mediocre literacy skills may easily disguise high intellectual capacities. For teachers, one possible indicator of under achievement is the discrepancy between the student's apparent verbal/intellectual capacities and their formal school work. A student who is always quick with an answer and idea in oral sessions but seems to struggle with written language, would be a typical dyslexic student.

CAUSES OF DYSLEXIA

Heredity is recognised as a significant factor in dyslexia, with at least 50% of dyslexic students having a first degree relative with dyslexia. Scientists are now beginning to identify the genetic code that is associated with dyslexia.

Dyslexia is a disorder in the processing of information. Reading, written language and arithmetic involve a complex interaction between listening, language, seeing, remembering and action. Deficits can occur in one or several parts of the circuit required for successful reading and writing. Fluent, accurate reading and writing require the rapid integration of many higher mental functions into one unified, complete process.

Recent studies using brain imaging techniques show that children with dyslexia may process some types of information in a different area of the brain to non-dyslexics. The neural connections that underpin successful learning may not have formed effectively, so that other areas of the brain, perhaps less well equipped to process the information, have to become involved. This means that a simple task such as sounding out and reading a word may need to be re-routed through alternative pathways, causing a slower and more difficult process, with a higher risk of error.

Dyslexic difficulties are not caused by poor teaching, problems with hearing or eyesight or family tensions (although of course these factors can make matters worse).

There is considerable ongoing discussion and debate amongst experts in the field, about the causes and the characteristics of dyslexia. In recent years, there has been recognition of the central role that phonological awareness plays in dyslexia.

Phonological awareness refers to the ability to recognise sounds within words and to manipulate sounds e.g. blend sounds together in reading or split words into sounds as part of successful spelling. Many dyslexic students are slow to develop adequate phonological awareness and may experience ongoing difficulties in this area.

A core difficulty for dyslexic students is in the development of automaticity. They may be able to perform the required skills, but only by putting in a lot of extra effort and working slowly and mechanically. Whereas a non-dyslexic student may recognize words quickly, and sound out unfamiliar words fluently, the dyslexic student struggles. Words that they may have seen or written many times before are handled like new words that have to be processed all over again, because they are not yet automatically recalled when needed.

A small percentage of dyslexic students will have difficulties in the visual memory system. They will have problems remembering sight words, have difficulties with accurate copying and will usually be poor proof-readers. Difficulties with visual recall of printed patterns will lead to a slow acquisition of the link between sounds and written letters at the beginning stages of reading, and a heavy reliance on phonics once the basic letter-sounds relationships have been mastered.

EARLY RECOGNITION AND INTERVENTION

Dyslexia is best managed by early recognition and early intervention. When learning takes place, the brain makes connections which create pathways. As the pathways develop the brain recognizes previous information when it is encountered again and is able to respond more accurately. We know that young children's brains are 'plastic' and resilient, and more able to make connections than older, more mature brains. However, there is never a time when intervention is not appropriate when it is needed. The human brain constantly creates new connections and pathways right through to old age.

The earlier a child is recognised with dyslexia, the more time there is for intervention and the better chance there is of preventing long-term failure and the emotional damage that this can cause. Early intervention also gives the dyslexic student the best chance of being able to keep pace with their peers and prevents them from falling too far behind. Late intervention often means that there is a lot of catching up to do.

Dyslexic students often make only slow progress in their school work. A lot of effort from teachers, parents and the student may yield only small gains, and progress may be inconsistent. What a dyslexic student learns one day is often forgotten the next, so that forward progress is constantly undermined by the loss of earlier learning, which has to be repeated over and over again. This in turn can undermine a student's confidence and motivation. It also means that what is taught needs to be very carefully selected, so that the high level of resources that are needed to achieve success are not wasted on a trivial or irrelevant learning outcome.

Dyslexic students learn best when they have tasks that build on previous successes and where there is a lot of structure in what they are doing. Dyslexic students usually need frequent, explicit feedback on how they are doing, so that areas of success or difficulty can be clearly understood.

Intervention is most effective if it is given early, and if it is individualised, to meet a dyslexic student's unique pattern of difficulties and strengths. Because learning occurs when connections are made within the brain, it is important that the activities given are specifically targeted to develop the pathways that underpin successful learning. This means that if a student has difficulties in sounding out words then activities should centre around the skills required for this task.

This book provides many practical examples of activities that can be used to develop the skills required for successful learning.

LEGAL ISSUES

In most countries students with dyslexia are protected by anti-discrimination legislation in education. Throughout the world dyslexics in schools, colleges and universities have the right to special consideration in their study programs and especially in their assessments and examinations. This means that they cannot be excluded from educational services or educational programs on the grounds of their dyslexic difficulties e.g. problems with reading or spelling, provided that they can fulfill the essential requirements of the course of study.

Legislation usually requires that adjustments and accommodations are provided in such a situation. This book gives many practical examples of the types of support which are appropriate.

Some, but not all, countries have legislation to ensure that dyslexics are provided with an individualised educational program.

The failure of school systems or individual teachers to recognize dyslexia (thereby denying a student access to appropriate programs) is a complex legal issue. In a society which places increasing emphasis on legal accountability, litigation seeking compensation for the disadvantages caused by failure to recognize and remediate dyslexia is likely to become much more common in the future.

ELIGIBILITY FOR FUNDING IN SCHOOLS

There is no international standard or convention with regards to funding within schools for dyslexic students. Countries vary in the degree of legislation which they have in place, to ensure that schools provide appropriate programs for dyslexic students. Whether or not there is legislation in place, individual educational agencies (LEAs, school boards, education departments etc.) usually do allocate resources to meet the needs of dyslexic students. Generally speaking funding is more readily available to students with multiple disabilities such as dyslexia combined with Attention Deficit Disorder or for those students who have severe dyslexia.

ELIGIBILITY FOR FUNDING FOR PARENTS

There is no international standard or convention with regards to funding for families of dyslexic children. Most developed countries have some form of child allowance, which may be available to parents of a dyslexic child, especially if the dyslexia is severe and/or coupled with other difficulties.

DYSLEXIA OVER THE LIFE SPAN

Dyslexia is a lifelong condition. However with appropriate intervention, particularly at the early stages of schooling many of the difficulties can be substantially improved. The accepted treatment is individualised remedial teaching designed to address dyslexic difficulties. This is generally combined with a range of compensatory strategies within the classroom.

MYTHS ABOUT DYSLEXIA

Myth
'It will click', or 'The child will grow out of it', or 'They all learn at their own rate'.

Fact
Students who do not establish adequate proficiency in reading and writing skills in their first year of school are at risk of long term difficulties unless they are identified and provided with appropriate remedial assistance.

Early detection makes the treatment of reading difficulties much easier and helps to avoid the loss of confidence and motivation that can easily build up if problems are not recognised promptly. We know there are many early warning signs which tell us which students are at risk of long term learning difficulties.

An intervention program should be commenced as soon as difficulties are detected.

Myth
All students with reading difficulties are dyslexic.

Fact
There are other causes of reading difficulties, such as lack of appropriate teaching, emotional disturbance, general developmental delay or language disorder which need to be excluded before a remedial program is started.

A comprehensive assessment is essential to establish the cause of the difficulties before an appropriate intervention program can begin.

Myth

The teaching of phonics is old fashioned.

Fact

Recent studies show that phonics are vital in the teaching of reading, especially for those students who have reading difficulties. What other students pick up easily dyslexics may need to be taught step by step, over and over again e.g., the letters and their sounds, common spelling patterns etc.

Many dyslexic students have difficulties in phonological awareness (the ability to break words down into sounds or to blend sounds into words). Studies show that training in this skill can improve reading.

Myth

All dyslexics see print upside down or in reverse and write in mirror image and are confused about left and right.

Fact

While some dyslexics do have difficulty with reversing letters and mirror writing, many do not. Current research indicates that many dyslexics have subtle difficulties with language and sounds. Laterality (how the left and right hemispheres of the brain organise information) was thought to have a direct link to dyslexia. In the light of more recent studies we realise that laterality is extremely complex and that there are many factors as yet not fully understood.

Myth

If you have dyslexia nothing can be done.

Fact

Whilst learning may take a lot of extra hard work, there is much that can be done. Firstly the dyslexia must be properly diagnosed by a specialist (usually a psychologist) who has expertise in the area. Then a teaching program can be tailored to the individual's particular pattern of strengths and weaknesses. Ongoing review and monitoring of progress is important.

Myth

It is damaging to label a child 'dyslexic'.

Fact

The term 'dyslexia' helps to eliminate other common negative labels such as 'lazy', 'low intelligence' etc., which often lead to a sense of relief for student and parent alike.

Once a student is diagnosed as dyslexic, parents and teachers can access the extensive body of good quality information on dyslexia, which can lead to significant improvements in the approach used to teach literacy skills.

The label 'dyslexia' may entitle the parent and school to additional funding from Government agencies. In addition, it may well entitle the student to special provisions in educational programs, special support and special provisions in examinations.

The label of 'dyslexia' also means that the dyslexic usually is protected by disability discrimination legislation.

Myth
If the student was better organised, better behaved and tried harder then there would not be a problem.

Fact
We know that some (but by no means all) dyslexic students do have motivational, confidence or social problems as part of their learning difficulty. They may have poor social judgment, may be impulsive and badly organised, or have communication difficulties. This may mean that they do not get on as well as others and may think that they are 'dumb'. The student may try to cover up difficulties by acting the clown, becoming disruptive or switching off.

A dyslexic student may try their best with their school work, only to be told, perhaps time and time again that they should try harder. Facing constant frustration and failure often leads to loss of motivation and self confidence.

Myth
If the dyslexic student just practices more, the problem will be solved.

Fact
'More of the same' will not remediate deficits in the complex processes involved in reading and written language. Specific difficulties need direct, planned intervention. Many suggestions can be found within this book to assist in planning an appropriate program.

Myth
Dyslexia means that you will never be able to get a good education or employment.

Fact
Universities, colleges and schools can all make provision for people with dyslexia to study successfully.

Myth

In the old days everyone was taught to read and spell well.

Fact

There have always been people (often highly talented and famous) who have had difficulties with reading and spelling. Nelson Rockefeller, Thomas Edison, Albert Einstein and Agatha Christie are all said to have been dyslexic.

Action plans for the successful management of dyslexia

- Given that most classes of 30 children will have about 3 dyslexic students, consider screening the entire class for literacy difficulties that have not previously been detected

- Give all students the opportunity to work in oral, practical and written modes and compare the differences in their performance. The dyslexic student may outperform others in the practical or oral modes but perform poorly in written mode

- Actively look for intellectually bright students who, although performing at an adequate level are underachieving. Use both verbal and non-verbal tests, and avoid using tests which require high level reading or writing skills

- Parents are often the ones who see a very bright youngster at home becoming a 'dumb' student at school. Check with parents of all students, about whether they feel their child is performing up to their expectations

- Given that dyslexia is often an inherited condition ask parents to indicate whether there is a family history of dyslexia in any situation where there is concern about a student's progress or performance

- View students with poor literacy skills (untidy writing, inaccurate copying, poor spelling, reluctance to read) as possible dyslexic students rather than students of limited ability

- View students with behavioural problems as possible dyslexics who have become discouraged and negative because of learning difficulties

- View students who are very disorganized as possibly dyslexic (with or without Attention Deficit Disorder)

- Value oral and practical work, and make sure that all students have the opportunity to demonstrate their skills in tasks which are free of literacy requirements

- Be aware that disability discrimination legislation applies to education programs and services and that the requirements of the legislation will impact on your school's policy and practice

- Ensure that all dyslexic students have appropriate remedial assistance (see later chapters of this book)

- Ensure that all dyslexic students have appropriate adjustments and accommodations to allow them to access the curriculum (see later sections of this book)

- Ensure that all dyslexic students have appropriate adjustments and accommodations when they are being assessed (see later sections of this book)

- Keep informed of current developments in the understanding of dyslexia by joining appropriate organizations, reading professional journals and information sources (such as the websites for the British Dyslexia Association and the International Dyslexia Association) and attending conferences

- You will find a wide range of suggestions contained in the following pages of this book, please refer to them to develop action plans for successful learning for your students

READING

READING, DYSLEXIA AND SCHOOL WORK

Reading difficulties are one of the most obvious signs of dyslexia. Whilst a student may eventually acquire basic reading skills the process is much slower and needs much more teacher and parent input than would normally be expected.

Reading is a complex process. At the beginning stages the student has to recognize individual letters and remember their sounds. These sounds have to be blended into whole words, and the whole words have to be understood as part of a sentence. The student draws on their underlying knowledge of language structures to anticipate the next word in a sentence and to understand what has been read. In the English language the student also has to recognize some words as irregular, and know these words by sight.

A young dyslexic student may be very slow to pick up the basics of letters and their sounds and may have great difficulty in blending the sounds together to make a word.

> **John, now a very successful businessman remembered his early years at school**
>
> *I used to look at the other kids. They just knew those words. I used to think to myself 'How do they do that?' I'd pick up the book and look at all those letters–they just didn't make any sense to me–just black letters all over the page. My mother and my teachers worked and worked with me, and sometimes I could just sense their frustration. I had one teacher who used to tap her pencil while she waited for me to read the next word–guess she hated my reading session as much as I did!*

Dyslexic students find it difficult to remember the appearance of words that they may have seen many times before. This means they have to stop, 'sound out' or guess by using context over and over again.

Bright dyslexics may have good reading comprehension but poor accuracy.

When a student has reading difficulties they will have problems with many aspects of their school work. They may not be able to read well enough to understand worksheets (even though they could do the tasks easily if they could read what to do). Their reading may be painfully slow. Researching for a project, will be a challenge. Limited reading skills make locating appropriate reference material very difficult indeed. Difficulties in reading an examination paper may damage the student's chances of demonstrating their knowledge of a topic.

A bright dyslexic's way of coping with silent reading

Well, you see you have to sit there and look like you are reading, so I count letters…it's really good…your eyes move just like you are reading…mostly I do the alphabet…and the first page I count how many 'a's I can see, then on the next page how many 'b's…it gets a bit boring really……

Action plans for successful learning

- Monitor all young readers, and take special notice of those who seem to need more input and make slower progress than their peers

- Be quick to pick up early reading difficulties to prevent loss of confidence and frustration at the very early stages of reading

- Regularly review all students to check on the development of their reading

- Do not assume that because a student does well with silent reading comprehension that their accuracy is equally good. Check reading accuracy as well as comprehension

- Ensure that there are plenty of tasks that do not depend on good reading e.g. interviews, videos, films, audio tapes and practical learning can all be the starting point of a valuable learning activity

- Offer alternative assessment tasks that do not depend on skilled reading e.g. oral tests instead of written tests

- Make suitable reading materials available for students whose interest level is in advance of their reading skills

- Avoid asking students to read out loud in class unless they wish to do so

- Provide an appropriate reading program to improve skills

- Modify curriculum materials so that although the content remains the same, the level of reading required is reduced by using easy to read words, short sentences etc.

- Check the reading difficulty level of curriculum materials by using the readability statistics option on your computer grammar check.

- Make worksheets and homework sheets physically easy to read.

> Use good quality photocopies
> Print information in a large font (minimum point size 12)
> Use a clear font such as Arial or Comic Sans
> Leave plenty of space around each item
> Draw attention to particularly important information by
>   graphics and special effects
> Use tinted or off white paper
> If handwriting has to be used write in clear print

- Allow extra time for completion of set work. This may necessitate reducing the work load to avoid increasing the overall time a student is expected to work

- If extra time is not practicable then shorten a question paper to take account of slow reading speed. If the question paper starts with easy items and moves onto more challenging questions get the student to do alternate items and then go back (if there is time) to fill in missed questions, so that they get a good mixture of easy and difficult items

- Provide a reader to read essential information to the dyslexic student

- Provide support so that the reading is shared between the dyslexic student and a more skilled reader

- Supplement printed materials with demonstrations, verbal explanations, diagrams

- Provide essential information in an alternative form (diagram, audio tape, video)

- When a project is set provide a resource folder to help the student get started (get capable students to donate their background resources for next year's students)

   Copies of relevant reading
   Abbreviated notes
   Highlighted text, diagrams
   Illustrations
   Video
   Suggested topic headings

- Put curriculum materials on disc or scan text books, information sheets, worksheets or test papers into the computer and use text to speech software. If writing for text to speech software

   Use punctuation at the end of headings and bullet point items
   Use numbered items to ease navigation
   Use short sentences and paragraphs
   Use lower case letters

- Use a text scanner that can scan individual words and give a read out

RECOGNIZING COMMONLY USED WORDS

When dyslexic students read they often lack automatic word recognition. This means, that almost every word they come across has to be worked out from scratch, over and over again, each time it is encountered.

Printed words are usually easy to remember when they are visually distinctive and have an interesting meaning, *spaghetti, elephant, zebra* all look distinctive and have real meaning and most young readers find them quite easy to remember.

In contrast words such as *where, here, he, they, the, then* etc are visually similar, have no interesting meaning and are very difficult to recall. As adults we sometimes think these words should be easy because they are used so often. For dyslexic students they often prove to be the most difficult and frustrating words of all. Remember that matching and recognising words are easier tasks than reading words at sight.

Action plans for successful learning

- Introduce beginning readers to sight words by matching and recognizing activities before reading is required. Matching to sample is the easiest level, reading words is the most difficult

Match to sample (sample in view)

This teaches the student to discriminate between print patterns

Choose about five different words and write each out five times on separate cards. Spread the cards out on the table. Choose one word card and hold it up for the student to see

Say *This card says 'house'. Find another card that says 'house'*

Match to sample (sample hidden)

This teaches the student to hold a mental image of a printed word

Choose about five different words and write each out five times on separate cards. Spread the cards out on the table. Choose one word card and hold it up for the student to see.

Say *Look at this word. It says 'who'. Remember what it looks like because I am going to turn it over.* Place the card face down and say *Find another card that says 'who'*

Recognise a named word

This teaches the student to link a printed word with a spoken word

Choose about five different words and write each out five times on separate cards. Spread the cards out on the table

Say *Find me the word that says 'out'. Find me the word that says 'my'*

Read words at sight

This is the most difficult level. The student is asked to remember a print pattern from previous learning and to name the word

Choose about five different words and write each out five times on separate cards. Spread the cards out on the table

Point to the words in turn and say *What does this word say?*

- Use games such as Word Lotto, Word Snap and matching games to help develop quick, automatic recall of words

- Use flash cards regularly to promote quick automatic recall of printed words

> Remember that words like these are really hard to tell apart and difficult to remember
>
> *where   here   he   the   we   what   were   there   is   they   their   she   and*

- For the emergent reader use match to sample sentence building to teach word recognition and sentence structure

  Write an interesting sentence on a strip of card. Make an exact duplicate of the sentence and cut it into individual words. Give the student the words cards from the cut up strip

  Say *Look, this sentence says 'It is my birthday on Saturday. You put your cards down so that they say 'It is my birthday on Saturday'*

  Encourage the student to use the complete sentence as a guide. Make sure that the student reads back their sentence once it is complete

- For the student who already knows a few sight words use *sentence building* to strengthen word recognition and sentence structure. This activity helps to constantly revise core sight words.

  Have a set of words on individual cards. *Magnetic Poetry* (available from many book stores) provides interesting word sets that will stick to fridges or any metal surface

  Say *Put these cards together to a make a sentence.*

  You can either dictate a sentence or the more advanced student can choose words from the set to make their own sentence

> Try words like these to build a young readers confidence
>
> *tyrannosaurus rex   pizza   Sesame Street   giraffe   chocolate   banana*
> *Scooby Doo   whopper   elephant   STOP   spaghetti   Lion King   Lego*

- Make personal reading material using the student's name and relating to their interests, but include the difficult to remember sight words

- Use reading materials that are in a well structured series to provide repetition and controlled level of difficulty

- Avoid relying on randomly selected books (even if the books are sorted according to difficulty). Select books that control the introduction of new words and consolidate previously introduced words

- Use reading books which have supplementary material such as workbooks, parallel readers, flash cards etc. associated with them

- Make one reading book the core of a range of literacy activities such as

     Home made readers which reintroduce words from the reader
     Sentence building to give extra practice with the new words
     Word games to build familiarity with the new words

- Give daily reading practice

LEARNING LETTERS AND SOUNDS

Learning letters and their associated sounds is the beginning point for successful reading and spelling. Sometimes delay in this learning is due to poor memory but more often it is due to underdeveloped phonological awareness. If the student does not recognize individual sounds in words then learning printed symbols to represent those sounds makes no sense at all. The first step is to provide training in awareness of sounds in speech and spelling. *(pages 37-44)*

Learning the relationship between letters and sounds is a difficult type of learning because neither the individual sounds nor the individual letters actually mean anything at all to the young student.

Teacher holding up the letter **S** *Ben, what does this letter say?*

Ben *I never heard it say nothing*

Learning letters and sounds is a complex task of integration between the language channel (which handles the sounds) and the visual or visual motor channel (which handles the written letters).

Action plans for successful learning

- Before you can teach the link between printed letters and sounds you must make sure that the student can at least tell the initial sounds in words. If they cannot do this then continue to work at basic phonological awareness activities *(see page 38 onwards)*

- Match letters to pictures on the basis of initial sounds

- Use more than one word/picture for each letter sound to teach that **S** is not just associated with *sun* but also goes with *snake, sand, sausage etc*

- Use a multisensory approach so that students learn through sight, touch and sound. Students can practice making their letter shapes by tracing the letter with their fingertip in wet sand, icing sugar sprinkled on a flat surface, steam on a window or polenta or sugar sprinkled on a baking tray. It is important that the student is encouraged to simultaneously say the sound as the letter is being formed.

- Do not teach letters that sound similar at the same time. Avoid introducing **S** and **Z**, or **m** with **n**, as they are so easily confused

- Do not teach letters that look similar to each other at the same time. Avoid introducing **f** and **t** or **b** and **d** at the same time as they are so easily confused

- Ask parents and classroom volunteers to use only sounds to avoid confusion between letter names and sounds

- Teach letters and their sounds in stages

Matching

You will need a set of letters which has duplicates for each letter. Hold up a letter and give the sound. *This is* **S**. *Find me another* **S**. Students with a very limited letter-sound knowledge should be given only two or three letters to choose from to make their match. As they gain confidence they can be given more letters to choose from

Recognize

This is slightly harder, because the student is not given a sample or its sound to start with. Instead, the adult scatters some letters in front of the student and asks *Find me* † (or whatever letter the adult wants to work on). Once again, young students who have not got a full repertoire of letters and sounds established should only be given a few multiple copies of the same letter within their set, so that they can have repeated practice

Read

At this level the student is not given a sample and is not given a target sound to find. Instead they are shown a letter and asked *What is the sound of this letter?*

Record

This is the hardest level of all. The student hears the sound and is asked to write it down *Write down the letter that makes the* m *sound*

- Provide an illustrated alphabet strip or chart to help the dyslexic student remember the letters that match each sound

USING PHONICS IN READING

One of the most common characteristics of a dyslexic student is difficulty in using phonics for reading. The process of linking letters with sounds, and then stringing the sounds together to make words, is a challenging one for the dyslexic student.

The student may be very confident in giving the sound to each individual letter, but when they have to blend the sounds, they are lost e.g. they may sound out *skin* but think that the word is *sick* or *snick*

All readers have to master the skills of recognizing clusters of letters within long words. These 'chunks' are easier to work with than strings of individual letters.

It is usually essential for the dyslexic student to have intensive and explicit instruction with regards to phonics. This type of input is often required for a number of years until the basics are fully established.

Action plans for successful learning

- Assess the student's current ability to sound words out using phonics and decide if remedial input is required. If so establish an appropriate starting point

- Use one of the highly structured phonic programs especially written for dyslexic students. It is essential that the program teaches phonics in an explicit and highly structured way. The International Dyslexia Association and the British Dyslexia Association have information about recommended programs. Well respected programs include Hickey, Orton Gillingham and Spalding

- Select a reading program that has a high phonic content and which is structured to provide graduated practice in phonics

- Work from easy to difficult phonic patterns

Suggested sequence of instruction

1 Three letter words in a consonant-vowel-consonant pattern sound
   hot jam mud top
2 Four letter words, where two letters slide together to make a sound
   flag step best tick
3 Four letter words where two consonants make a new sound
   shop thin chat when
4 Four letter words where a vowel and a consonant make a new sound
   corn fowl warm quit
5 Four letter words with a final '**e**' *mice, date, kite, made*
6 Three and four letter words where two vowels make a new sound
   rain out loud meat
7 Silent letters *knee gnaw gnat know*
8 Five letter words where three letters slide together *strap scrum strip judge squid*
9 Five and six letter words where four letters make a new sound
   fight dough nation
10 Longer words that combine two or more of the above patterns
   jumper beach sprawl tribe
11 Prefixes, suffixes and compound words *predict disagree truthfully household*

- Teaching a dyslexic student requires considerable skill. If possible arrange for a suitably qualified and experienced teacher to plan and implement an appropriate program

- Teach groups of words with the same phonic clusters together to consolidate awareness *pain rain gain* or *gate hate mate fate*

- Use nonsense words as well as real words to give additional practice and to challenge phonic skills

- Work from short words to longer words. Do not use long words to teach basic phonics. If teaching **st** use only four letter words such as *stop, step, list* and not words such as *steamer, string, beast*. The longer words have additional phonic challenges which will confuse the student

- Give auditory blending activities. The student listens to strings of sounds and says the word

Say *I am going to say some sounds slowly. You put them together to make a word*

Sample words
t – ap
s – un
m – a – n
b – e – g
fl – a – g
st – a – mp
cr – a – sh

If this is difficult for the student use picture prompts. The adult sounds out the names of objects which are illustrated on a card. The student selects the picture that goes with the word they have just heard

- Give modelled practice. The adult prepares a list of words. The adult sounds out the first word and says the whole word *c-u-p, cup*. The student is then asked to repeat the process in exactly the same way (sounding the letters and then saying the whole word). The adult then moves to the next word on the list and repeats the procedure. Once the list has been worked through, then the student is asked to go back to the beginning again and sound and blend for themselves

- Give plenty of guided practice (the student practices and the adult guides) in the use of phonics for reading

- Once the basic phonics have been mastered teach the rules for syllable division and provide plenty of explicit practice in this skill. Use both real and nonsense words to develop skills

- Return to the basics frequently for checking and (if necessary) revision because dyslexics readily lose previously established skills

- Use analogy reading to encourage the development of being able to use one word to help with another *If this says 'tease' then that word says........ (please)*

- Accelerate word decoding with phonics by giving short, intensive *'sound and say'* drills. Word cards are dealt out quickly and the student is asked to *sound and say* as fast as they can

- Write down pairs of words that look quite similar *girl grill, red read, pair pure.* Name one of each pair for the student to find *Which one says grill?*

READING FLUENCY

Once the dyslexic student has mastered the skills in sounding out new words and recognizes most commonly used words at sight, there may still be significant problems in developing fluent, confident reading. Reading may be slow and stilted, so that meaning is often lost and reading becomes a real chore. Although this lack of automatic reading is often part and parcel of the dyslexic difficulty, jerky hesitant reading can sometimes be a habit stemming from earlier difficulties.

> **Margo a dyslexic adult recalls her schooldays**
>
> *Usually I never got asked to read to the class, but one teacher she got me reading the prayers all the time 'Margo', she'd say 'You read the prayer, it sounds so reverent the way you do it' I reckon it was only because I was so darned slow…couldn't have gone any faster if I tried!*

Many dyslexic students can read reasonably successfully, but reading still takes a long time. Some words may have to be puzzled out and text may need to be read several times over before it is fully understood. Dyslexic students often fail to finish set reading because they run out of time.

Hesitant reading can also be a characteristic of a student with a word finding problem. If so then a similar hesitancy will probably be occasionally noticed in ordinary conversation.

Action plans for successful learning

- Give intensive, supported practice to improve reading skills and speed

- Select reading books that have a large percentage of familiar words

- Select reading books that follow from each other in a series, so that core vocabulary, style, font type etc. are consistent and the introduction of new words is controlled

- Encourage the re-reading of previously enjoyed books

- Pre read new books to the student so that they have an overview and understand the story before they start to read for themselves

- Encourage the student to look through a new book to familiarize themselves with it before they start to read

- Use modelled reading where the adult reads a sentence or small section with expression and the dyslexic student copies the modelled reading as closely as possible

- Use a highlighter pen to mark up each sentence into phrases and give the student guided practice in reading in phrases instead of words e.g. instead of *Once – upon – a – time – there – was – a – wicked – king – who – had –a beautiful – daughter* read *Once upon a time - there was a wicked king - who had a beautiful daughter*

- Select books which are short in length but of high interest to the student

- Audio tape the student reading and let them listen to the playback. Record until they feel comfortable with the recording. Keep the first tapes for the student to hear how much they have improved

- Use timed reading. The student prepares, rehearses and practices reading the same passage until they are fluent and accurate. Time the first read through and note time taken and errors made. Repeat the process aiming for reduction in time and errors. The student might like to calculate their reading rate (words per minute)

- Try choral reading where a small group of students rehearse a poem or short story as a dramatic presentation. The readers read in unison and rehearse until fluent and expressive

- Introduce humour, drama or excitement into individual reading

  Rehearse reading a comedy routine of good jokes or stories, maybe perform them to friends

  Practice for a part in a short play, and perform the play for fun (have the script stuck around the stage or use big cue cards to give the performers their words)

  Practice reading a story and then audio tape it for another student to enjoy

  Read a news flash like a TV news reader with the auto cue on the screen of a computer

  Practice reading a book at school to take home and read fluently to parents, siblings or grandparents

- Assess the student's reading both in silent and oral modes. Poor oral reading may be due to word finding difficulties not reading difficulties

- Avoid making the student read aloud in front of peers

- If reading aloud in front of peers give time and support for rehearsal

- Reduce the volume of reading required by highlighting important sections, or setting only selected chapters, chapter summaries or shorter sections to be read

- Share reading with a skilled reader so that the reading process is speeded up by taking turns

- Use paired reading, where the dyslexic reads in tandem with a skilled reader, the skilled reader sets the pace a little faster than the dyslexic's usual speed. This can help with the transition from word by word reading to fluent, expressive reading

- Use books on audio tape for the student to read along with (take care that the book is an exact match for the printed text and that the speed is appropriate)

- Allow sufficient time for essential reading to be completed properly

- Avoid overloading the student with reading requirements

- Allow the student extra time in tests and examinations to take account of slow reading speed

- Provide supplementary information such as diagrams to convey information more quickly

READING COMPREHENSION

Dyslexic students often have quite good reading comprehension provided they can read the text fluently and accurately enough to be able to focus on the meaning of the words. Poor comprehension is often associated with books that are too difficult to read.

Some dyslexics do have subtle language problems that interfere with reading comprehension.

Action plans for successful learning

- Obtain advice and support from a speech therapist if it is felt that the student has general language difficulties

- Monitor the readability of books, check that any book the student is attempting to read is within their range of reading skill

- Tell the student a brief summary of the book before reading begins to ensure that the student has an overview of the theme or story line

- Choose books with plenty of illustrations to support comprehension

- Encourage re reading the book, the first read through is to work out the actual words, the second read through is for understanding

- Pre read the book to the dyslexic student before they read it for themselves

- Talk about the book and ask questions. If the student's comprehension seems uncertain offer choices between two alternative options *Did they go to the park or the beach?* instead of *Where did they go?*

- Ask the student to locate information to develop comprehension *Find the part that tells us how Tom was feeling*

- Check that the book's language is not too advanced for the student

- Get the student to devise reading comprehension questions for other readers to encourage them to think about the meaning of what they are reading

- Delete words from text and get the student to predict the missing word to encourage reading for meaning

- Get the student to draw a cartoon style strip to retell the story

- Teach the student how to use the words of the question to guide their answer. If the question is *Why did Harry hate the building?* the answer could begin *Harry hated the building because...*

- Ask the student to select the best answer to comprehension questions from a choice of two or three possible options. *Why did the chicken cross the road? a) Roast chicken tastes better than fried chicken b) Because she wanted to get to the other side c) Because she was afraid of the dark*

- Teach students to listen to key words in questions. *A why* question usually has a *because* answer. A *where* question often has *in, on, by, near* or *at* in the answer. A *when* question usually has *after, before, when, on* or *at* in the answer

SUSTAINED READING

For the dyslexic student reading can be a real struggle and just a few lines can take a lot of effort. Dyslexic students often find sustained reading very difficult. They can read for a short period of time but quickly become exhausted by the effort required. This means that they often find it difficult to enjoy a book. They read a little and then stop because they are already tired, so that they do not really get into the book and begin to enjoy it.

Quick onset of fatigue when reading can also be related to visual difficulties not connected with dyslexia

Action plans for successful learning

- Arrange for eyesight to be tested

- Do not expect skilled reading when the dyslexic student is already tired

- Help the dyslexic student to structure their reading into short, manageable sections

- Locate books that have short chapters but interesting stories or information

- Assist with reading by sharing the load, take turns to read a paragraph or a page each

- Start off a book by reading the first chapter or two to get the dyslexic student interested and keen to read on

- Find books that follow an already familiar story e.g. where the student has already seen the video

- Find a time for reading when the student is free from distraction

VISUAL TRACKING

To track along a line of print and then drop accurately to the next line of print, and continue tracking word by word is a very refined skill. Some dyslexics have difficulties with this. In its extreme form, it would be described as ocular-motor dyspraxia.

Some students with scanning difficulties will attempt to scan along print by moving their head and keeping their eyes static. Others will constantly lose their place when reading or copying.

Action plans for successful learning

• Arrange for an assessment by an optometrist, or opthalmologist with specific reference to ocular movements (scanning).

• Use a piece of plain card to underline the line of print which is being read.

• Provide enlarged text, which is double spaced.

• Rest the book on a sloping surface rather than on a flat surface

• Put reading material on a computer, and use the cursor as a pointer

• Project text onto a flat vertical surface at a distance, to allow for less precise eye movements

• Simplify work sheets, so that the text is well spread out and clear to read

WANTING TO READ

Dyslexic students often avoid reading whenever possible, perhaps hiding or 'losing' books to avoid reading practice. Some students even claim to be ill, volunteer to do errands or behave badly to get themselves outside of the classroom when it is time to read. Some dyslexic students become anxious and agitated when they have to read, others may become tearful or angry and upset. This may mean that reading practice is limited which further compounds the problem. Dyslexic students still acquiring basic reading skills should read to an adult every day.

The emotional and social consequences of dyslexia are discussed in detail in Chapter 8.

Action plans for successful learning

- Teach don't test. Give as much help as the student needs to read successfully. Tell the student unfamiliar words, help with sounding out, read alongside the student to get through difficult parts

- Make sure that the book being read is at a reasonable level of difficulty. The student should be able to read at least nine words out of ten for comfortable reading

- Set up a relaxed atmosphere for reading. Curl up on a couch or comfortable chair. Have a supply of treats reserved only for reading time. Enjoy the book by looking at the pictures, talking about associated topics, as well as actually reading the words

- Suggest that the student uses a signal (such as raising a finger or tapping on the table) to indicate that they need help with a particular word

- When listening to the student read allow a silent count of four seconds if they get stuck. Then simply sound the word out and say the word *l-ou-d, loud* and allow the student to continue reading.

- If the word will not sound out then just say the word and let the student continue reading

- If the student makes a mistake but the word they use makes sense let them continue without comment

- If the student gets in a muddle take them back to the beginning of the sentence and start them off again. Read along with them if they need extra help

- Some adults let their own anxieties or impatience show through, which in turn makes the dyslexic student very nervous when they read. In this situation find an alternative person to listen to the student read

- Keep reading sessions short and let the dyslexic student know how long the session will last so that they do not feel trapped for an indeterminate time *We will read until the buzzer goes. Then we will stop*

- Make sure that adults keep track of reading books and monitor how often the student reads. Good communication between home and school is important to prevent avoidance tactics

- Reading without preparation can be very threatening. Allow the dyslexic student to preview the book and say when they are ready to read

- Do not assume that the dyslexic student will actually read during class reading time. Make this a time for reading to an adult or give reading based activities such as crossword puzzles, multiple choice quizzes, cloze activities etc to give interactive reading practice

- Find books that although easy to read have a high appeal for the student. Joke books and books of amazing facts are often popular because a short piece of reading really can be enjoyed

- Record favourite TV shows to be watched after reading is completed

- Make reading practice a set homework assignment in place of another, less important task. Do not make the student do reading as an extra chore, on top of the regular work load

- Model enjoyment in reading. Let the student see that adults read for information and pleasure

- Create a reward system for reading, so that the hard work involved has a tangible, positive outcome

- Make a lucky dip. Write rewards on slips of paper and put them in a jar

  Get a chocolate frog from the box
  Skip your turn washing up
  10 minutes extra TV before you go to bed
  Your choice of dessert tonight
  50 pence for you

- Draw a grid of 10x10 squares. Each square represents 1 minute of reading. If the student reads for 4 minutes then they colour in 4 squares. Small rewards can be given for completing each line of 10 squares and a larger reward can be given when the square is complete (100 minutes of reading). For really reluctant readers put in some bonus squares. When they reach or exceed the bonus square that session's minutes are doubled

- Get a group keen to read by making reading a fundraiser for a favourite charity or school project. Make sure the dyslexic student has a reasonable goal e.g. other students may get sponsored by the book, the dyslexic student might get sponsored by the page

- Allow reading time to be offset against household chores e.g. reading for 20 minutes cancels out one washing up duty

chapter 3

LANGUAGE AND DYSLEXIA

LANGUAGE SKILLS

AWARENESS OF SOUNDS IN SPEECH AND SPELLING

WORD FINDING

LANGUAGE SKILLS

Most contemporary definitions of dyslexia describe dyslexia as a fundamental difficulty with language based skills. The neurological process of linking auditory information (spoken words) with visual information (printed words) is extraordinarily complex. It is not surprising that difficulties sometimes occur in the development of the pathways and connections that underpin the ability to use language, to read and to write.

Research studies consistently demonstrate that most dyslexic students have a disorder in their ability to process language. This difficulty may often be at a very subtle level, but nevertheless it has a profound impact on the ability to read and write.

We also know that children who are late learning to talk, or who have disordered early language, are at higher risk of having dyslexia than children who have had no early language difficulties. Indeed, dyslexia may sometimes be seen as a residual of earlier language problems. More overt language difficulties may clear up through maturity and therapy, but subtle processing problems often continue.

We know that young children who have a history of recurrent ear infections seem to be at greater risk of dyslexia than children who have had few, if any, ear infections. The probability is that there is already a risk factor, but the disruption of the child's auditory processing development in the critical early years leads to continued difficulties as the child grows older.

It is also known that speech, language, and phonological difficulties have a genetic component. It may often be that several children in the same family, or several members of the same family, all have similar language related learning difficulties.

Action plans for successful learning

- Ask parents about earlier speech and language difficulties as part of your school enrolment procedure

- Ask parents about their child's history of ear infections, grommets and intermittent hearing difficulties as a pre schooler as part of your school enrolment policy.

- Ask parents about their family history of speech, language and literacy difficulties as part of your school enrolment procedure

- View any students with a history of speech and language difficulties as 'at risk' of literacy problems in their early years of schooling

- Monitor students with a history of speech, language or hearing difficulties for continuing, more subtle language difficulties (such as delay in the development of phonological awareness) which may impact on their learning at school

- Give all new school entrants a basic screening test of phonological awareness and language skills

- Arrange for an assessment by a speech pathologist and/or a psychologist who specialises in language/literacy disorders if you are concerned about a particular student

AWARENESS OF SOUNDS IN SPEECH AND SPELLING

The process of acquiring spoken language is based on the ability to hear segments of speech (phonemes) within words and the ability to manipulate these sounds. Babies babble as they practice the phonemes in their language, older children love to play with phonemes by making up nonsense rhymes. This ability to recognize and deal with phonemes will play a central part in the early stages of literacy acquisition. Children with early difficulties in establishing these basics will be delayed in their readiness to work with phonemes when they start to learn to read and write.

Phonological awareness is the ability to recognize individual sounds within words and to recognize the number and position of these sounds. Phonological awareness is a critical beginning point for correct spelling. Without recognizing the sounds within words, the student cannot use letters to represent those sounds to write a word down. The student has to be able to recognize the number of sounds within the word, and the order in which those sounds occur. They also, of course, have to know the letters which represent those sounds.

Sensitivity to sequence of sounds is also a very important aspect of phonological awareness. Difficulties with sequencing sounds leads to problems with pronunciation e.g. *hostipal* instead of *hospital*. In turn this will lead to spelling problems.

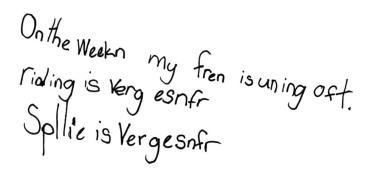

This student has not yet developed adequate phonological awareness to underpin accurate spelling. She has written

On the weekend my friend is coming over.
Reading is very easy
Spelling is very easy

Action plans for successful learning

- Start teaching phonological awareness activities at the oral level, followed by 'hands on' physical manipulation of letters, and finally writing words.

Oral

At this stage, nothing is written down at all. The aim at this level is to help the student become aware that speech is split up into words and that words can be split up into sounds (phonemes).

- Word counting. The adult says sentences and phrases and the student has to count the words

Say to the student *How many words do you hear?*

Sample phrases and words
Poor bear
Brightly coloured beads
Pitter patter pitter patter
I can see stars
I love chocolate pudding
Who has been eating my porridge

- Finding the missing word. The student has to listen to a list of words and notice the missing word. Start with two words and then increase the list length

Say to the student *Listen to the words I say: flowers, apples, spoon. I am going to say them again, tell me which one I miss out : apple, spoon*

> Sample word lists
> *window (dog)*
> *(flower) laugh house*
> *road book pen (cup)*
> *boy (girl) baby mother*

- Rhyming words. The student recognizes and produces rhymes

Level 1: Rhyming sequences. Say to the student *Tell me the word that comes next, rat, bat, sat,*

> Sample sequences to complete
> *Rose, nose, those, . . .*
> *Head, red, led, . . .*
> *Tree, me, he, . . .*
> *Hit, fit, pit, . . .*

Level 2: Rhyming words. Say to the student *Tell me a word that rhymes with house*

> Sample words for rhymes
> *play*
> *top*
> *inner*
> *socks*

- Clapping syllables. The student listens to words and recognizes syllables

Say to the student *We are going to clap and count syllables. Sun has one syllable* (clap and say *sun*), *sunshine has two syllables* (clap on both syllables of sunshine)

> Sample words
> *leg*
> *rocket*
> *sister*
> *toy*
> *caravan*

- Phoneme deletion. The student listens to words and deletes phonemes

  Say to the student *We are going to say words and then take part of the word away. Say 'sunshine'. Now say it again without the 'sun'*

> Sample words
> *teapot without the tea*
> *telephone without the phone*
> *classroom without the class*
> *cup without the* c
> *room without the* m

- Play 'I-Spy'. Select three or four items, which have distinct initial sounds. Place the items on a tray and play at 'I-Spy' using letter sounds (not names) Say *I spy with my little eye something beginning with* 's'

> Sample items for tray
> *pencil flower box soap*
> *horse cow duck farmer*
> *apple banana cracker marshmallow*

- Give riddles that have an initial sound as a clue

> Sample riddles
> *An animal that you can ride. It starts with* d *(donkey)*
> *A fruit that is yellow. It starts with* b *(banana)*
> *Something that you wear. It starts with* h *(hat)*

- Talk about words, and identify the first sound in spoken words *What is the first sound in bell?*

- Give the student two or three individual consonants written on separate cards. Say three letter words and ask the student to point to the sound they heard at the start of each word

  Listen to this word. What sound comes first? Show me the letter

- Choose a word. Take it in turns to think of another word that has the same sound

- Recognize initial sounds and match to the correct letter. Give the student two or three individual consonants written on separate cards plus one blank card. Place these cards on the table. Give the student a set of pictures.

  Say *Put these pictures by the right letter. See here is a house, that goes with the* h *card. This is a bird. There is no* b *card so we will put it in on the blank card*

- Once the student is accurate with the initial sounds, start to work with final sounds in three letter words

- Play I-Spy with final sounds *I Spy with my little eye something that ends with* t

- Recognize final sounds and match to the correct letter. Give the student two or three individual consonants written on separate cards plus one blank card. Place these cards on the table. Give the student a set of pictures.

  Say *Put these pictures by the right letter. Here is a cat. Cat ends with* t *so that goes with the* t *card. This is a dog. There is no* g *card so we will put it in on the blank*

- Give the student two or three individual consonants written on separate cards. Say three letter words and ask the student to point to the sound they heard at the end of each word

Say *Listen to this word. What sound comes at the end of the word? Show me the letter*

- Middle (medial) sounds are the hardest and these are introduced once the student is confident in recognizing first and final sounds

- Give the student two or three individual vowels written on separate cards. Say three letter words and ask the student to point to the sound they heard in the middle of each word

Say *Listen to this word. What sound comes in the middle? Show me the letter*

- Saying sounds in words. The student has to identify each sound in order e.g. the sounds in wet are *w-e-t*

Say *Tell me the sounds in this word.* Start with simple CVC (consonant vowel consonant) words

Samples of CVC words
wet
tom
hip

Samples of CCVC words
flag
twin
step

Samples of CVCC words
best
mend
mint

Concrete

Whilst working at the oral level, begin to introduce plastic letters (lower case), to help the dyslexic student to learn to manipulate sounds and place them correctly in order.

- Word building. Choose a three letter word e.g. *pig*. Get only the letters needed for the word.

  Say *Look, I can make the word pig with these letters, p – i - g, pig*

  Once you have made the word scramble the letters and move them towards the student

  Say *Now you make the word 'pig'*

  Encourage the student to say the sounds as the letters are placed in order. If they are not sure what to do put the first letter in place and let them complete the word

- Once the student is confident do not give an example. Just provide the letters needed for a word and get the student to place the letters correctly. Always encourage them to sound out the word as they place the letters

- When the student can build three letter words with the letters provided give them a larger set of letters to choose from e.g. for a three letter word such as *hat* give five letters such as *h,j,a,e,t* so that the student has to make a choice about what sounds are needed

- When three letter words are mastered move to four letter words with a consonant blend e.g. *flag, twin, best, mend*

- Swopping sounds. The student builds a word with plastic letters and then has to take one letter away and replace it with another to make a new word

Say *Make the word 'pig' with the letters. Change 'pig' into 'wig'. Take one letter away and find another to make 'wig'*

Sample words (initial sounds)
Change dad to mad
Change cat to hat
Change tin to pin

Sample words (final sounds)
Change dog to dot
Change hit to him
Change peg to pen

Sample words (middle sounds)
Change him to ham
Change cat to cut
Change tip to top

WORD FINDING

Many dyslexic students have difficulties with 'word finding'. The words that they need are within their vocabulary, but they experience difficulties in 'finding' those words when they are needed. The student with the word finding difficulty may often seem to talk quite a lot, but close listening will show that they may be substituting words, hesitating and using 'fillers' such as, 'ah', 'ur', and 'you know'. As pre-schoolers, they may have been slow at learning to name colours, and may continue to have difficulties in naming things quickly. Many studies show that difficulty in rapid naming is one of the most common characteristics of dyslexia.

Looking for missing details in pictures- easy to find, but hard to name if you have a word finding problem

The stick thing (handle of a broom)
The bit...the thing that you stand on (the step of a ladder)
The watch what goes round thing (the watch band)
You know the thingy...the thingy...that's a thingy bit that you pull (the handle on a drawer)

Students with word finding difficulties will often seem to perform erratically in the classroom. They will put their hand up and will be eager to answer, but when asked to make their contribution 'forget' what they were going to say.

Word finding difficulties are often much worse when the student is tired or upset. In disputes or upsets with other students the student with the word finding difficulty may have significant problems in negotiating verbally, and may be more likely to communicate physically, and have more difficulty in explaining to an adult what has happened.

Students with word finding problems are also likely to have problems with reading fluency. They may recognize the word and understand what it means, but experience difficulties 'finding' the right word to say out loud. The process of word finding has to be quick and automatic for fluent oral reading to occur. Students with word finding difficulties may often have particular difficulties with oral reading, and may be much more accurate when they read silently.

Action plans for successful learning

- If word finding difficulties are observed, arrange for a speech and language therapist to assess and advise

- When the student is speaking, give them plenty of time to 'find' words that they need

- If the student offers an answer but then cannot remember what they were going to say offer them a way out *Were you going to say the animal in the story was a camel?*

- Rehearse assertive statements such as *Stop it, I do not like it* or *You are breaking the rules* to give the student with word finding difficulties phrases that comes easily even when upset

- When an upset has occurred give the student time to calm down. Let the student tell their side of the story without interruptions from others

- Encourage the student to write down their answer before they put their hand up to answer a question

- Do not judge a student's arithmetic by their oral answers, as word finding difficulties may disguise their capabilities

- Check reading accuracy and comprehension using silent reading and oral reading. A student with a word finding difficulty may be much better at silent reading

REMEMBERING HOW TO SPELL WORDS

Dyslexic students frequently have major difficulties in remembering spellings that they have learned. They may well get a high score in a weekly spelling test, but their overall spelling in their own writing is poor. They can learn spelling 'parrot fashion' for a test, but do not retain this spelling. Many dyslexics follow a 'learn and forget' pattern of spelling (learn the words for Friday, forget them by Monday, start learning the new set and repeat the process time and time again).

Dyslexic students with this type of memory difficulty often have to reinvent the same word over and over again each time they try to use it in their own writing. The spelling patterns which they have learnt have not progressed to automatic recall.

Although accurate spelling is important we have to remember that quality writing does not depend on correct spelling. Dyslexic students who are made to feel overly anxious about their spelling may restrict what they write to avoid spelling errors. They may seriously reduce the overall quality of their work in doing so.

Action plans for successful learning

- Separate out good writing from good spelling. Always give credit for creativity, expressive vocabulary, interesting information, innovative ideas, good thinking, evidence of good research etc

- Sort words out into those that can be learned by word building using phonics and those words that are irregular

Action plans for successful learning of phonically regular words

- Check that the student can recognise sounds in words. To begin phonic spelling the student should be able to tell the individual sounds in three letter words. *(see page 38)*

- Check that the student knows how to write the correct letter for each sound.

- Provide an alphabet strip on the desk so that the dyslexic student can refer to this when needed. Each letter needs a picture prompt to help with the link between sound and letter

- Start by building a word with plastic letter *(see page 43)*. Get the student to sound out the word until they are confident they can remember it, scramble the letters and ask the student to write the word down. Encourage the student to repeat the sounding out process to assist with the recall of the phonic pattern

- Teach the student to always try to say the sounds before they start to write a word. This helps to reinforce the development of phonological awareness and significantly increases spelling accuracy

See page 23 for a suggested sequence for the introduction of phonic patterns

- When teaching phonics for spelling, focus on the blend being taught. For instance, if teaching *ou*, keep to three and four letter words e.g. *out, loud,* and do not introduce longer words such as *shouted* because these words have additional complexities which make it harder for the dyslexic student to hear the sounds correctly

- When introducing new words always emphasise the phonic structure of the word. Teach the student to split the word into phonemes (units of speech) to assist in recall. For example instead of trying to rote learn the eight letters in *spelling* learn the three phonemes *sp-ell-ing*

- Use nonsense words to give extra practice at detecting sounds in words

- Do not teach spellings in theme groupings e.g. words to do with the circus, as there is not enough consistency in the spelling patterns for dyslexic students with phonological difficulties

- Teach spelling rules that can be applied to help with accurate spelling

- Constantly revisit previously taught phonic families to consolidate recall

- Constantly revisit taught spelling rules to consolidate recall

Action plans for successful learning of irregular words

- Use rainbow writing. Write a word in large clear print and have the student write over it time and time again with different coloured pencils to reinforce the correct spelling pattern

- Target just a few words at a time. Write the words clearly on a piece of card. Place the card in a prominent place. Then have a fun challenge with the student, to see if they can always spell the target words correctly. Give positive reinforcements for correct spelling e.g. a jelly bean each time the target word is used and written correctly

- Make a desk dictionary- this is a sheet of firm card which has an alphabetical list of words which the student uses often but has difficulty spelling. The card can also have a few interesting personal words and phrases to support more risk taking in writing

- Get the student to make themselves a small personal dictionary (address books are good to use) to make their own personal word list

- Give multisensory practice. Encourage the student to say the letters as they are written down. Physically writing, or typing, a word is an important way of learning how to spell irregular words. With practice we create a motor memory of how to write a particular word

- Use the Look-Copy-Cover-Write-Check routine to practice irregular words

  Look: Look at the word, notice the pattern of letters, close your eyes, try to remember how the word looks. Find groups of letters that go together
  Copy: Copy the word down. Say the letters to yourself as you write
  Cover: Cover the word and try to remember what it looks like
  Write: Write the word down, say the letters to yourself as you write
  Check: Check your spelling. If you got it wrong write it out correctly, highlight where you went wrong before and then go through the Look-Copy-Cover-Write-Check routine again

- Get the student to write the word with finger painting

- If students are learning linked script and need to practice use spelling words for writing practice to double up the benefits (spelling practice and handwriting practice)

- If students can already do linked script encourage them to practice their spelling using it rather than printing (linked script gives a more integrated motor memory than printing)

- Get the student to make a design incorporating the correct spelling as part of the graphics

- Practice spelling the word correctly in context. Dictate a series of short sentences, all containing the target word. To begin with provide a sample of the target word so that the student can refer to it as they write. Subsequent practice sessions using a new set of dictation sentences containing the target word can be given, without a sample of the target word in sight

- Teach *old way, new way* look at the way the student spells the word and teach the difference. *In the old way you used 'h', in the new way you leave the 'h' out*

- Use memory aids such as *we went* for *went* or *ants running everywhere* for *are*

- Use the following mastery based learning approach

- **Step 1**

  Choose 3 or 4 words which are suitable for the student you are working with. Make sure that the student can read the words, understands their meaning and is likely to use them frequently. Words that are never used by the student will not be retained beyond the teaching/testing phase.

  Alternatively, test through a basic sight vocabulary list until you find three or four words that the student cannot spell. Use these as your starting point.

- **Step 2**

  Get a set of small blank cards. Write the words you have chosen for your spelling program on the cards (one word per card). Each time the student spells the word correctly they tick the reverse of the card.

  You will also need three containers to keep the cards in. Label these *workshop deposit store*

- **Step 3**

  Pre-test the words which you intend to teach. Put any words that the student already knows in the *store* container.

  Put words which are not yet known in the *workshop* container.

- **Step 4**

  Teach the words which are in the *workshop* container, until the student is able to spell them correctly on three consecutive teaching sessions. Put a small tick on the back of the card each session to keep track of how many times the student has been able to spell it. When there are three ticks on the back of the card, put it in the *store* container.

- **Step 5**

  Move on to the next list of words, making sure that you choose a suitable number, so that your child will not be overwhelmed with a large number of words. Go through the same process again, allocating the new words to the *workshop* or *store*

- **Step 6**

  Start each new session by revisiting *workshop* and *store* containers. Mark each card with a tick, to show that it was recalled correctly. When six ticks have accumulated, the words can be moved from *store* into *deposit*

- **Step 7**

  Keep working on new words, introducing them through the *workshop* container. The word is moved from *workshop* to *store* once it has three ticks

- **Step 8**

  About once a week, go through the *deposit* container. Any words which have been forgotten go back into the *workshop* container to get three new ticks. Then they can go back into *store*

  Keep ticking each time the student is able to spell the word.

- **Step 9**

  Any card which has nine ticks on it can be discarded. The student may enjoy being able to tear the word card up or cross the word off a list to show that they have well and truly mastered it.

  Note: If the student seems to be going through lists of words quickly increase the number of words in each new list. If the student is finding it difficult introduce new words more slowly

  Whilst nine correct attempts are usually enough to show that the words have been mastered, some students, particularly those with learning difficulties need additional practice. They might for instance have four ticks at each stage, before the word card moves on to the next level

WRITTEN LANGUAGE

Many dyslexic students have subtle language difficulties. They may have difficulties at the word level (poor pronunciation), or they may have difficulties at the sentence level (poor structure and organisation of their sentences). In some cases, a bright student may appear to be less capable than they really are, because of expressive language difficulties.

> One day there was a cleaner cleaning in stead of cleaning he was looking abват he sciencfes were doing Some work on the moter.

This ten year old student has an IQ of 140

Action plans for successful learning

- Any student with a problem in the structure of either spoken or written language should be seen by a speech and language therapist with expertise in dyslexic disorders

- Write sentences and then cut the sentences into words. For older students you can use phrases. The cards are then arranged to reform the previous sentences or make new sentences. Younger students work with short, simple sentence constructions. Older students work with complex sentences

- Give a sentence which has a word missing. The student is asked to repair the sentence by inserting an appropriate word

- Give a paragraph that has a sentence missing. The student is asked to repair the paragraph by inserting an appropriate sentence

- Give sentences that have to be arranged into a logical sequence

- Give words and phrases that have to be included in a sentences *then he went, but, after all, because*

- Give cartoon strip pictures to prompt the story line in sequence

- Provide a picture (or series of pictures) with useful vocabulary alongside, to provide scaffolding for writing

- Give a list of prompt words that help improve written expression *even though, meanwhile,*

- Teach planning skills using mind maps (charts and diagrams)

- Use a suitable software program to organise ideas for written work

- Some students find it easier to visualise a piece of written work as a film or TV broadcast to get the structure sorted out. Use a story board to turn ideas into written work

- Give additional scaffolding such as subheadings to assist in the structure of a big piece of work

- Look at how the experts do it. Take a magazine or newspaper article of interest to the student and discuss how the piece is structured *How does the author introduce the topic? What would a skeleton plan of the article look like?*

- Read stories to the student to improve their awareness of sentence structure and story structure

- Read stories and ask the student to fill in the missing word when you pause. This can also give the adult insight into the student's difficulties with language

- Allow a verbally fluent student to dictate ideas to a scribe

- A verbally fluent student who has difficulty getting their ideas down on paper might use an audio tape to record their ideas. They then type up from the tape.

- A verbally fluent student who has difficulty getting their ideas down on paper could use voice recognition software

- Provide formal, explicit instruction in written grammar. There are numerous activity books and textbooks available for individual and classroom use

- Use workbooks intended for students of English as a second language to provide useful additional practice in written expression

- Older students can use predictive software on their computer. This software predicts the next word in their sentence as they type

- Older students also benefit from using software which can turn text into speech The software program will allow the student to actually hear what they have written and this often helps correct poor written sentence structure

- Older students may need additional editorial support, to polish their written drafts

- Check the setting of the grammar check on the computer that the student uses to ensure that it is set for an appropriate writing style

- Give simple dictation to improve the link between language and writing. Give the text in phrases to help the student to move from word by word writing to fluent, grammatically correct writing

- Give a question plus about eight statements that are factually true and relate to the topic. Ask the student to set aside those statements which do not relate to the question being asked, even though as statements they are correct

PROOF READING

Dyslexic students often have significant difficulties in proof reading. The dyslexic student may have no way of telling whether words are right or wrong. Dyslexic students often pick correct words as errors and rewrite them. They overlook genuine errors.

Using a dictionary is of little help. The dyslexic student may spend a lot of time looking up words that are correct and fail to check words that are wrong. Because they are unsure of how to spell words they may be unable to find the word they need in the dictionary.

It is dangerous to dive into a swimming pool because if you don't now the depth, you may injure youre skull, or spine when you hit the bottem.

Example of a dyslexic's proof reading. Notice how she has 'corrected' words that were right and ignored errors.

Action plans for successful learning

- Encourage the use of an adult to function as an editor/proof reader

- Allow work to be produced on a word processor, with spellchecker and grammar checker

- Investigate advanced software options for enhanced accuracy e.g. predictive word processing

- Encourage the student to classify the type of error that they usually make e.g. a constant error such as *aer* for *are,* incorrect word endings etc. This makes proof reading a little easier

- Allow extra time in tests and examinations for proof reading

- Do not penalize spelling errors unless accurate spelling is a key requirement of the task

- Do not expect the student to use a dictionary to check words. Dyslexic students often think that correct spelling is wrong and use valuable time searching the dictionary only to find they were right all along. They will not check words that they believe are correct. Looking up words in a dictionary is difficult if you do not know how to spell the word

- Use a computer program that can read back what the student has written, to assist in proof reading

COPYING

Dyslexic students often have great difficulties in copying things down accurately. They may copy their spelling words down from the board but have errors before they even start to learn. It may mean that they do not get homework requirements down accurately, and so they get home without a clear record of what they are supposed to do.

Copying can also take a very long time, as well as being inaccurate. The dyslexic student may have serious trouble in keeping up with the rest of the class.

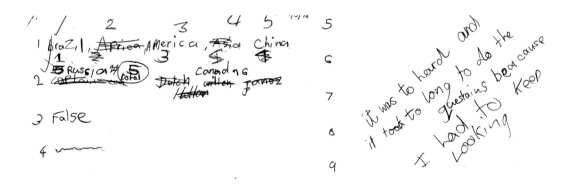

Notice how much better this student's writing is when he is writing his own words and not trying to copy from the board.

The dyslexic student will often only remember one or two letters at a time. They write down two letters, look back to the board and find their place in the word they are copying, write down the next one or two letters and repeat the process over and over again. This is a slow and very frustrating process. If the student has to turn around to copy the process is even more difficult.

Older dyslexic students can find it very difficult to access curriculum materials if they have to be copied down. It is especially difficult if the teacher talks while the students are copying.

Dyslexic students are also inaccurate at copying because they have a limited repertoire of words that they can spell. Whereas a student who can spell most of the words they are copying, can easily read two or three words and then write them down from memory (with correct spelling, because they already know how to spell the words) the dyslexic student cannot do this.

Action plans for successful learning

- Avoid unnecessary copying

- If copying is essential ensure the student is facing the board and has an unobstructed view of the print

- Provide work sheets rather than have students copy out questions

- Provide handouts, photocopies of notes and printed information sheets

- Ask a fellow student to use a carbon to create a copy for a dyslexic peer

- Allow the dyslexic student to photocopy or scan a fellow student's notes

- Put essential information on a web site or computer network

- Allow extra time or shorten the task when copying is essential

- Teach the dyslexic student to break words up into manageable, meaningful sub-sections so that accurate copying is easier

- Where a student has to copy things down check the accuracy of what they have recorded

- In tests and exams where accurate copying is required such as maths, allow extra time

HANDWRITING AND BOOKWORK

All young students do of course have to acquire the basic skills of writing, as they start school. For some students this process is quick and easy but for many dyslexic students the process is slow and tedious.

Before a student can actually learn how to form letters, they must be able to not only control a pencil but also understand how to form various shapes. For instance, they must be able to create a smooth curve (necessary for the letters such as *o* and *c*) combine straight lines and curves *(n, m, u, b)* and diagonal lines *(y, x, v, w).*

Capital letters are easier than lower case letters because they are formed from less complex shapes (more straight lines, fewer complex mixes of curves and straight lines). However, it is important that younger students are introduced to lower case rather than upper case, particularly if they are likely to have problems with writing. Some dyslexic students use a mixture of upper and lower case letters. This may sometimes be to avoid letter reversals or may be due to poor awareness of the difference between the two types of letters and their respective uses.

Whilst some writing difficulties are due to muscle problems, most are caused by motor planning problems. Unfortunately whilst muscle problems very often improve quickly and easily with training, motor planning problems (caused by a dysfunction in the neurological pathway between the brain and the hand) are much less easily treated.

Although students do improve with practice there are some students who have ongoing and significant difficulties with handwriting despite expert therapy and huge amounts of practice. Severe handwriting difficulties are called *dysgraphia.* Dysgraphia is a recognized disability, and students with dysgraphia are usually eligible for special provisions when they take examinations.

The advice *Try harder-do better* can cause substantial frustration to the dyslexic student whose best efforts produce an illegible scrawl.

Dyslexics often have difficulty with sustained handwriting. The student can write very neatly for a short while, but after that their hand writing deteriorates very rapidly. In a classroom situation, this may mean that they write for a little while and then stop to give their hand a rest. This may look as if they are being inattentive or distracted. Sometimes a student's difficulties with sustained writing do not become evident until they start to take examinations. Writing for three hours can be an impossible challenge for some dyslexics, who have previously managed to get by writing in bursts of five or ten minutes.

Note taking can be very difficult for the student who has difficulties with sustained writing. Notes may be incomplete or illegible.

Word processing is often less neurologically challenging than handwriting. It is much less likely that there will be problems with sustained writing using a keyboard. However some dyslexic students find that typing is just as difficult as handwriting.

Dyslexic students often have to make a choice between speed and neatness. They can produce neat work, provided they work extremely carefully and slowly and take rest breaks. This of course is not an efficient way of producing work. If asked to rewrite untidy work, the student may struggle to even match the neatness of the first draft.

Dyslexic students often realise that it is easier to produce a short neat piece of work (with no rewrites) than to produce a lengthy, interesting but untidy piece of work (when a tedious rewrite is certain to be required).

Many dyslexic students have extreme difficulty with neatness. They may have memory difficulties and be poor at copying things down, and have to constantly look backwards and forwards between book and board. This in itself makes letters irregular and poorly spaced (because they are written one at a time and not fluently as a whole word).

Many dyslexic youngsters have problems with the spatial/perceptual aspects of book-work such as being able to organise print neatly on a page, space words evenly and write letters neatly. Some dyslexic students have trouble judging how much space they need for a particular word, so that they are constantly running out of space at the end of a line, or overcompensate and stop almost halfway across the page to make sure they have room for the next word which they then write on the next line.

Poor bookwork can cause enormous frustration to adults and students alike. This is particularly so when there is a high emphasis on neatness. Students do need to be reassured that neatness is not, in itself, a critical academic attribute.

Action plans for successful learning

- Beginning writers should use lower case not upper case. Parents of pre-schoolers should be reminded of this if they plan to teach their child to write

- Give tactile experience of letter formation. Spread icing sugar, shaving foam, polenta or any other tactile material on a flat surface and get the student to trace the letter shapes with their fingertip. The adult may need to place their hand over the student's hand to guide them to start with

- Experiment to find the best type of writing tool. Soft lead pencils, roller ball style pens or similar may give a smoother line and make writing easier and clearer

- Seat a left handed writer to the left of a right handed writer to avoid collisions

- Minimise unnecessary writing. Provide worksheets, printed handouts, rather than requiring the student to take notes

- Accept that writing which is neat will not be quick

- Emphasise that quality of content counts for much more than neatness

- Accept that the dyslexic may well produce work which is messy and untidy, even with the best effort

- Accept that neatness will deteriorate rapidly when volume or speed is required

- Make it clear to the student whether neatness or speed is required. Accept that the dyslexic may not be able to produce both neatness and speed simultaneously

- Encourage the development of good word processing skills. Rough drafts can be typed up, printed out, edited and reprinted

- Assess the student with oral rather than written tests

- Negotiate extra time in examinations for the student with writing difficulties

- Negotiate for the student to use a word processor instead of handwriting in examinations

- Allow for rest breaks when the student has a lot of writing to do

- Use a scribe to support the student with handwriting and typing difficulties

- Use voice recognition software for the student who has both writing and typing difficulties

- Do not require a dyslexic to rewrite messy work

- Provide someone to type up work if the content is good but presentation poor

- Write on alternate lines to allow space for corrections

- Provide scaffolding (pages with pre-printed borders with interesting coloured paper etc. so that good presentation is not dependent on the student's ability to be neat and tidy

- Mark separately for content and neatness. Give content a high percentage of the overall mark, neatness a much smaller percentage

- Give short tasks that the student can complete in the time available, to teach the student the skills of seeing a task through to completion

- Provide good seating arrangements. At an adult sized table, provide a small child with a box for their feet and a cushion for their back, so that they have firm support

- In school, make sure that table and chair are the correct height for the student and that they adopt a good writing posture (chair tucked in, feet firmly on the floor, back against the chair)

- Allow short cuts such as photocopying text and adding notes

LETTER AND NUMBER REVERSALS

Many young students reverse letters and numerals. Dyslexic students may continue reversing letters beyond the age of seven, and maybe even through to adulthood.

The problem in reversing letters and numerals is often caused by an error in the neurological pathway, which triggers the hand to make the letter movement. Whilst memory aids such as *The bat comes before the ball* can help, often it only adds to confusion for the dyslexic student This mnemonic depends on the student knowing *before* means to the *left* of the letter, and knowing left from right.

A more effective strategy is to use an existing neurological pathway that is already established for another letter.

Action plans for successful learning

- Teach **b** as an extension of the letter **h** (using the same neurological pathway). Start off with the **h** and continue the stroke round to form the **b**. The memory prompt for this can be *hubba bubba*

h b h b h b h b

- Teach **d** by using the existing neurological pathway for **a**. Start off with **a** and continue the vertical stroke upwards. The memory prompt for this could be *dad* or *add*

a d a d a d a d

- **p** is based on the neurological pathway for **n** The vertical stroke is extended downwards and the curve is completed (the memory prompt for this is *nipper*).

n p n p n p n p

- Give tactile experience of letter and numeral formation. Spread icing sugar, shaving foam, polenta or any other tactile material on a flat surface and get the student to trace the letter or numeral shape with their fingertip

MULTIPLICATION TABLES

THE LANGUAGE OF MATHS

SPATIAL AWARENESS AND MATHS

MULTIPLICATION TABLES

One of the primary disorders in dyslexia is difficulty in remembering sequenced information, such as multiplication tables.

Multiplication tables are challenging because they require good memory of basic number facts but also require the student to remember the sequence of individual items in the multiplication table. Many dyslexic students get in a muddle because they get lost when they are reciting their tables. They lose their place, skip items, or go back and repeat some items over again.

Dyslexic students may be paradoxical maths students, finding the easy arithmetic difficult, and conceptually challenging maths relatively straightforward. Difficulties in learning tables can cause considerable frustration, particularly if there is emphasis in the classroom on quick accurate recall of multiplication tables. Even very bright dyslexics may find this one of the hardest things of all to master. Other sequences which dyslexics have difficulties with include days of the week, months of the year, and sequences of words or sounds (e.g. spelling, telephone numbers or their own date of birth).

Action plans for successful learning

- Provide a calculator or number square when teaching a new maths process, to avoid memory difficulties interfering with new learning

- Do not estimate a dyslexic student's maths potential by only assessing arithmetic (recall of number facts, mental manipulation of numbers)

- Accept that inconsistency in recall of rote learned information is a common trait of dyslexic students

- Give the student a sheet with the tables written on it (with answers missing) so that as they recite their tables they do not lose their place

- Show students how, once they have learnt one or two multiplication tables, parts of the other tables have been mastered already

- Use number grids to provide multiplication table practice. This is often much easier than reciting a table all through

- Prepare a sequence of number grids of increasing challenge. Use a ten by ten square for all the grids and blank out the items not yet introduced

Levels of difficulty for times tables grids

Level 1: 1x, 2x
Level 2: 1x 2x 5x
Level 3: 1x 2x 5x 10x
Level 4: 1x 2x 3x 5x 10x
Level 5: 1x 2x 3x 4x 5x 10x
Level 6: 1x 2x 3x 4x 5x 6x 10x
Level 7: 1x 2x 3x 4x 5x 6x 8x 10x
Level 8: 1x 2x 3x 4x 5x 6x 7x 8x 10x
Level 9: 1x 2x 3x 4x 5x 6x 7x 8x 9x 10x

Sample of a Level 4 number grid

	1	2	3	4	5	6	7	8	9	10
1										
2										
3										
4				▨		▨	▨	▨	▨	
5										
6				▨		▨	▨	▨	▨	
7				▨		▨	▨	▨	▨	
8				▨		▨	▨	▨	▨	
9				▨		▨	▨	▨	▨	
10										

- For those students who already know more than 50% of their table introduce speed and accuracy drill to consolidate what they already know. Gradually build in the remaining tables as the student gains confidence and speed

- For students who are ten years and over who know less than 50% of their tables, accept that the effort and frustration involved in learning tables may not justify the outcome. Encourage the student to use a calculator or number chart instead

- When learning tables, remember that overlearning is essential for the dyslexic student. This means that they need to go over the same facts time and time again and also keep them in constant rehearsal to prevent them being lost

THE LANGUAGE OF MATHS

Many dyslexic students have difficulties with the language of maths. They understand the concepts, but get muddled up with the language. Language which relates to direction of operations may be particularly difficult. For example understanding the difference between *Take six from nine* and *Take nine from six*. Other mathematical terms such as *divided by, shared into, half of, twice as much, equals* can be very confusing for a dyslexic student.

Word problems may also be challenging for a dyslexic student who has problems with interpreting complex language.

A difficult question for a dyslexic student with subtle language difficulties

Question: *If you have three marbles in each hand how many marbles do you have altogether?*
Answer: *But I haven't got three hands*

Students with word finding difficulties may have difficulties producing the right answer quickly when put on the spot.

Dyslexic students with reading difficulties may have problems reading work sheets and other curriculum materials.

Action plans for successful learning

* Provide a language rich mathematical environment where the language of maths is used in an everyday context. Use play, travel, construction, cooking, gardening, games, sports and creative activities to promote the use of maths and the language of maths in a real life setting

* Check that the student really understands basic mathematical language such as *more than, less than, greater, shared, middle etc* when teaching new concepts

* Use consistent terminology when first introducing a new concept e.g. do not swap between *minus, subtract, take away* when first introducing subtraction

- Think aloud to give the student an insight into the internal language that accompanies the process that you are teaching *I've got to add 3 to 5. So I'll get three blocks and then I'll get five blocks. Now I will put them all in a line and count them to see how many I have got altogether. Now I can write the number here.* This helps the student with language difficulties to understand how other people think things through using internal language

- Give parents training sessions and information sheets so that they can use the same methods and the same language as the teacher

- Provide the older student with a glossary of mathematical words and phrases with worked examples where needed

- Provide reality based alternatives to explain maths terminology, e.g. *groups of* instead of *multiply* so that the student can read 3 x 2 as *three groups of two*

- Practice matching number sentences 8 + 5, 12 – 6, 5 x 4 to real actions with concrete materials such as plastic soldiers, animals etc (real items work better than counters) e.g. put a card with 5 x 4 down on the desk and have some toy soldiers on the desk

Say *Show me 5 x 4 with the soldiers*

- Show the student how to find key words in written word problems that give a clue to the process required. *Altogether* is going to need addition or multiplication. *How many were left* is going to need a subtraction

- When word problems are being given, encourage the dyslexic student to draw a simple sketch of the problem, to turn the problem into pictures not words

- Provide a reading buddy to support the dyslexic student in reading maths worksheets

- Write mental arithmetic questions down for the student who has language processing or memory difficulties

- Allow the student with a language fluency or word finding problem to write times tables rather than say them

- Look at the pattern of errors in the student's work, to diagnose problems in working method

- Ask the student to think aloud as they work so that you can hear the language and method that they are using

Sam was having a lot of trouble with his early maths. He was asked to show his teacher what he did.

He looked at the sheet of numbers and then looked away, half closed his eyes and touch counted his fingers. Then he wrote a number down. Asked what he had just done he said

'I counted like Sarah does'

Sam was just copying Sarah's behaviour and did not understand the internal language that was taking place when Sarah worked out the answer! Because he was only working with numbers less than ten he sometimes got the correct answer just by chance.

SPATIAL AWARENESS AND MATHS

Some dyslexic students have considerable difficulty with spatial awareness.

Understanding concepts that rely on an awareness of patterning can be difficult for the dyslexic student. These difficulties can range from tangible problems with shape and form through to more abstract difficulties in understanding order of magnitude *(is 46 larger or small than 53?)* and relative position of numerals *(is it 13 or 31?)* or being able to visualise a mathematical situation such as *If pencils cost £1.50 a box how many boxes can I buy if I have £9 to spend?*

Teaching fractions is often approached using diagrams. Unfortunately diagrams may confuse rather than help the dyslexic student with spatial awareness difficulties.

Understanding clock faces can be another major challenge for the student with spatial difficulties.

Another significant problem for dyslexic students with spatial awareness difficulties is in the direction of working in maths. Young students usually set out their work horizontally, working from left to right (the same direction as printed language).

However very soon working is arranged vertically, and worked from right to left. For the dyslexic student direction of working and sequence of actions can be very confusing

52	15	16	13
+35	+23	+71	+99
87	65	87	184

24	28	35	36
+32	+81	+53	+62
56	109	88	98

This student's working method was to add the top two figures together and record the total. She also added the bottom two numbers together and recorded that total. She was inconsistent in the order in which she did this and where she positioned her totals. In most of these examples she got the right answer with the wrong method!

Once regrouping and exchanging is introduced the student has to work from right to left, but also has to remember to work from the top to the bottom, and sometimes has to record diagonally (depending on the methods being taught)

Dyslexic students can find tasks such as copying numbers accurately, lining up columns of figures and writing numbers accurately very challenging.

Drawing geometric reasoning and geometric reasoning may also be a challenge for the dyslexic student. The student with spatial awareness difficulties often looks as if they have a coordination problem, when in fact they have reasonable physical control over their pencil, but run into difficulties in interpreting and reproducing complex spatial forms.

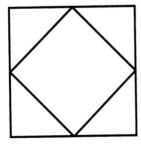

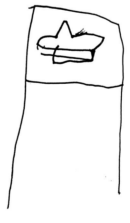

This is a dyslexic's copy of a spatial form.

Action plans for successful learning

- Give explicit teaching in setting out calculations

- Give visual prompts such as a green margin on the right hand side of the page to help the dyslexic student remember which side to start working from

- Provide printed worksheets where the calculations are already set out, leaving only the answer space blank

- Provide a 'recipe book' of step by step instructions and worked examples for each process

- Provide the student with squared paper to work on

- Try using lined paper placed on its side to provide vertical columns

- Provide a calculator which prints out so that maths students can show their working despite problems with neatness and setting out

- Teach how to write the numbers 13 to 19 with the memory prompt *You have to be one before you are thirteen* etc

- Teach reading the clock face in five stages

  Teach the student to tell the time using only the hour hand. This will obviously be an approximation *It's nearly half past six, it's nearly eight o'clock*

  Teach the student to read the minute hand   *quarter past, half past, quarter to.* Team this with the information from the hour hand

  Teach the student to read the minute hand to read the minutes from 0-30 *twenty past, five past.* Team this with the hour hand   *twenty past six, five past four*

Teach the student to read the minute hand for the minutes 30-60 as *twenty to, five to* (the mirror image of stage three when they read *twenty past*). Team this with the hour hand *Ten to six, twenty to three*

Teach the equivalence of *past* and *to* times. *Ten to six is the same as fifty minutes past five.*

- Teach fractions with language

  If we cut a cake into six each piece is called a sixth. If we cut a cake into five pieces each piece will be called a........

  If we cut a cake into eight each piece will be called a ....If we have two pieces of the cake we have two ....if we have three pieces of the cake we have...

  We write it down like this. We put 8 at the bottom, that tells us how many pieces the cake was cut into. Now we put a 3 on the top, that tells us how many pieces of cake we have.

  Look at this 5/8. How many pieces was this cake cut into......look at the bottom number. How many of those pieces do we have......look at the top number

chapter 6

MEMORY

MEMORY AND DYSLEXIA

MEMORY AND DYSLEXIA

Students with dyslexia frequently have difficulties with short term memory. Typically, they will show problems in retaining sequenced information such as multiple instructions, days of the week, multiplication tables, and the sequence of letters in spelling.

Dyslexic students' long term memory is often very good. Long term memory often depends on understanding, not parrot fashion learning. Dyslexic students may find it very difficult to remember how to spell a word from one day to the next, but have no trouble at all in remembering in detail a visit they made several years ago.

Dyslexic students often remember best when they are given information in more than one modality.

Dyslexic students often do not use internal rehearsal (saying something over and over in your mind) to help to retain information.

Dyslexic students often find it difficult to 'sift out' what they have to listen to and what they can safely ignore.

The mechanism of memory is complex, and irregularities can occur in processing, storage or retrieval of information. There are two important types of memory that underpin successful learning.

Listening (auditory) memory is needed to remember instructions and information, and to help process letter sounds when reading and spelling. Auditory memory also supports recitation learning such as multiplication tables.

Visual (eidetic) memory helps to store the appearance of words for reading, spelling, copying and proof reading.

There are various factors that make memory difficulties much more pronounced.

Concentration difficulties For short term memory to work we need to be able to concentrate on what we are trying to remember. Many dyslexics are easily distracted and so do not take in what is being said.

However poor short term memory in itself can mimic poor concentration. Dyslexic students may listen carefully but forget what has just been said. Diagnostically it is often difficult to tell what is happening in this chicken and egg situation. However, the combined impact of poor short term memory and difficulties with concentration is often a major source of frustration for dyslexics and their teachers alike.

Anxiety Memory is very vulnerable to disruption by anxiety. The physical consequences of anxiety (dry mouth, faster heart rate etc.) and the cognitive consequences of anxiety (agitation, preoccupation and distraction) make it significantly harder for short term memory to function properly.

Expectation of failure We know that expectation of failure often generates self talk, where the internal monologue of the student runs along the lines of *Oh, I'll never, ever remember this...This is so hard...I'm going to be in big trouble if I don't learn this quickly....* This type of thinking disrupts the memory process. The information which the dyslexic is trying to learn is pushed to one side by the negative internal speech which goes along with expecting failure.

Fatigue None of us find it as easy to learn things if we are tired. Dyslexic students are often very tired, because they have to work so hard during each school day simply to keep their head above water. This in itself will make rote learning more difficult for them, especially late in the day e.g. homework time.

Having too much to remember at once Dyslexic students often get overloaded with what they have to learn. Because they have difficulties with memory, each piece of learning takes more time and effort. This means of course that they cannot cope with the same volume of material as other students.

Not having the opportunity to consolidate learning We know that learning is most successful if a period of intense input is followed by a quiet time where the information can 'sink in' and consolidate. If a student has to learn new material without sufficient time for reflection and consolidation, then new learning will push out earlier learning before it has had time to be properly established in the memory.

Action plans for successful learning

- Teach memory strategies. Brain storm with the class to find out how other students remember things. Talk about mental rehearsal, organizing ideas, recording and planning

- Get the students to ask their family about how they remember things

- Ask the student to activate memory strategies *How are you going to remember this? What will be the best way for you to learn this?*

- Teach the student to use recall memory when studying. Re-reading notes activates recognition memory but does not help with recall. Use mini tests, draw diagrams, rewrite from memory to activate recall

- Give memory based work at a time of day when the student is not tired

- Break large memory tasks into a series of small tasks

- Make a clear distinction between definite requirements and optional activities. Dyslexic students with memory difficulties may not even attempt to remember apparent non essentials such as *I would like you to ask at home for some old magazines*

- Be explicit when things have to be remembered and try to activate the student's memory strategies. *This is priority one. Everyone needs to bring in their excursion slip by tomorrow, nine o'clock. Everyone stop right now and think about how you are going to remember this. Jack, what's your plan for remembering your slip?*

- Engage the student's interest by using the analogy of saving a document on a computer *Save this on your hard drive. Say it over to yourself to get it to save. Save it in your 'must do tomorrow' file. Open the file up to check its saved properly. Print it out and put the print out in your bag*

- Make sure the dyslexic student has time for rest and relaxation to allow fragile learning to consolidate

- Provide memory prompts such as dot points on the board to summarize instructions, provide checklists of routines

- Make sure that the dyslexic student feels confident and relaxed to optimize recall

- Avoid making scores from memory tests public knowledge, as this increases anxiety and reduces recall

- Avoid creating time pressure when recall is needed. Let the student work in their own time

- Allow a scribble pad to be used in mental arithmetic tests

- Let the student say when they are ready to be assessed to allow them enough time to prepare and to help reduce anxiety

- Give mental arithmetic and spelling tests 1:1 so that the adult can pace the questions to suit the student

- Allow plenty of time for rote learning

- Encourage students to use mnemonics (memory prompts) to help with recall. Ones they make up themselves often work best

- Encourage the student to make notes to compensate for poor memory

- Encourage the dyslexic student to ask for information to be repeated if they have forgotten it

- Prioritize what must be learned so that the dyslexic does not expend valuable time and energy on low priority memory work

- Keep instructions short and clear. Long strings of instructions may need to be broken up, so that only one instruction is given at a time. The student follows through the first instruction, and then the next instruction is given

- Emphasise the sequence of the instructions *First finish your worksheet*, **then** *tidy your desk* **and then** *you can get on with your poster*

- Instead of just saying instructions, give a demonstration, draw a diagram or picture or use a tangible way of showing what to do. Pin up a worksheet, put the waste bin on display, hold up a partly completed poster

- Tell the student the number of things they need to remember *There are three important things you need to remember. Number one, you must start a clean page. Number two, write in pencil. Number three, copy the date from the board. Remember, three things: clean page, pencil, date*

- Get the student to monitor the number of things they have completed. *You have to do four things. Number one, you need to clean your teeth. Number two, you have to put your clothes in the basket. Number three, you have to feed the dog. Number four, you need to put your lunch box in your bag.*

  Here are your four marbles. Put one in the jar each time you have finished a job. I want to see four marbles in the jar by the time I've done this washing up

- Use checklists or tangible reminders for the student to physically monitor what they have to do. Items are crossed off the checklist and tangible reminders (such as adhesive notes) are discarded once the task has been done

- Provided the dyslexic student is able to read sufficiently well, back up any verbal information in written form such as dot points on the board or a printed list of instructions to take home

- It is important that you have the dyslexic's attention before you give important information. *Everyone stop what they are doing and listen carefully*

- Signal when you are about to give out important information. Try to make it interesting to catch the students' interest. *News Flash! We have just heard from our reporter in the front office that the dates for the camp have been agreed*

- Vary the way classroom instructions or information are given. Get a student to read out what is required, draw the instructions, mime from your written list or give it in rap form

- Give the student a reason for listening carefully *This is a short cut for your homework*

- Impose a thinking time after an instruction has been given *Everyone just take a minute to think over what I have just said.* Then repeat the information once more

- Impose thinking time to encourage recall of previous instructions. *It is Thursday tomorrow, so stop and think what is special about Thursday. Before we go home let's just take one minute's thinking time. Think through everything you need to have in your bag for tonight's homework*

- Encourage repetition of what has just been said *Just let me check that I told you all the details, tell me what you have to do*

- Many students who have memory problems also have concentration and organisation difficulties, so read the next chapter on Concentration for many more ideas

chapter 7

CONCENTRATION

QUIET INATTENTIVENESS

DISTRACTIBILITY AND IMPULSIVENESS

PHYSICAL RESTLESSNESS

POOR ORGANIZATION

CONCENTRATION

Dyslexic characteristics such as poor auditory processing can easily mimic concentration difficulties.

Any student (dyslexic or not) can have medical problems such as sleep disorders, minor forms of epilepsy, fatigue etc which can impair the student's ability to remain focused. Many students with concentration difficulties also have problems with memory (see Chapter 5).

Some youngsters seem inattentive and poorly motivated because they are anxious, depressed or have other emotional difficulties or social problems.

Very bright dyslexics may also be suspected of having poor concentration because they are bored, even though they are finding the basic chores of learning difficult.

Many students with dyslexia also have concentration difficulties (ranging from mild to severe) and some may be diagnosed as having Attention Deficit Disorder (with or without hyperactivity). This means that you may be working with a student who has not one, but two disabilities (dyslexia and ADD).

Good management is always the first priority in addressing the needs of the dyslexic student with concentration problems.

A cognitive behavioural approach is the core of a good management program for concentration difficulties. This means students are helped to become aware of their own concentration style and to shape their own behaviour through awareness, planning and self monitoring.

Adult understanding, positive encouragement and patience are also crucial in successfully managing concentration difficulties.

Medication can sometimes have a role to play, particularly when the student's concentration difficulties are so severe that even with careful, positive management, their inattentiveness still interferes with their learning.

QUIET INATTENTIVENESS

Some students sit quietly 'in a world of their own'. Often they are very slow at completing tasks and often forgetful and disorganized. Because of inattentiveness they need frequent reminders to get started and stay on track. They may waste time getting started or take too much time on minor elements of a task, such as colouring in the title page.

Action plans for successful learning

- Refer the student to an appropriate specialist (paediatrician, psychologist, neurologist) for medical assessment if the student's inattentiveness causes severe problems in school

- Check that the level and pace of the schoolwork is at the appropriate level for the student (consider the possibility that the student might be bright/bored and dyslexic)

- Ask questions so that the student begins to understand their problem for themselves. *I didn't get started quickly enough so I haven't finished yet. I think I was day dreaming instead of getting the task done. I spent too much time on the fiddly bits and ran out of time for the important part of the task. I didn't have the right equipment on my desk*

- Involve the student in planning ways to overcome the problems of inattentiveness. *I can ask my friend or my teacher to remind me to concentrate. I can start on the most important part first. I can get started right away. I can get ready in good time. I can write a note to myself*

- Let students share ideas about how to stay on task *I keep reminding myself to keep working. I keep telling myself to stay focussed. I go as fast as I can. I try not to do anything else until I have finished. I set my stop watch and see how long it takes me*

- Encourage the student to self monitor their concentration and to let you know how they are going *Today I got all my things ready for maths really quickly and I was nearly the first student to get started on the worksheet*

- Ask the inattentive student to nominate a classmate as their pace maker. The student undertakes to try to equal or exceed their pace maker's work output

- Give the student frequent quiet reminders to stay on task

- Provide short pieces of work and explicit time limits

- Make instruction as interesting as possible (use colour, drama, music, humour, demonstrations etc)

- Allow extra time for work to be completed

- Give explicit training in seeing one task through to completion without a break

- Prioritize work so that the student gets started on the most important piece of work first

- Use visual prompts such as gold stars to remind the student of what is important

- Use short cuts to minimize the time taken on a piece of work

- Get the student working against the clock, or a timer

- Play games such as Snap where vigilance and fast reactions are needed

- Allow for some activities where a quiet, reflective approach is appropriate

- Give the student explicit, positive feedback for attentive behaviour. Give tickets *You are working well. You finished on time.* These are placed on the student's desk as appropriate and can be traded off for small rewards

- Older students who daydream or 'drift' off task, may need a 'prompter' in important examinations, to make sure they stay on task

- Use checklists to help the student remember an organization routine. For example stick a list of the morning reminders to the bedroom mirror. You will probably have to remind the student to look at the list

DISTRACTIBILITY AND IMPULSIVENESS

Many dyslexic students are easily distracted and impulsive. Punishments and rewards do not have much effect because the student does not stop and think about consequences before they act.

Many dyslexics with and without ADD will make 'careless' errors. A dyslexic student will probably find copying from the board, correct spelling and proof reading difficult, even with good concentration. Obviously a student with both dyslexia and ADD will have a lot of trouble with neat accurate work.

Action plans for successful learning

- Refer the student to an appropriate specialist (paediatrician, psychologist, neurologist) for medical assessment if the student's distractibility and impulsiveness cause severe problems in school

- Ask questions to help the student understand their own distractibility and impulsiveness. *I didn't stop and think...... I forgot to read the instructions.........I wasn't watching what I was doing......I answered before I had time to think...*

- Help the student to devise and implement strategies for managing impulsive, inattentive behaviour *I need to stop and think before I answer..... I have to remember to read the instructions.... I have to tell myself to listen carefully... I need to write it down and put it where I will remember it....I have to remind myself to concentrate*

- Encourage the student to self evaluate their concentration and impulse control and to tell you about their successes *You know when Billy was messing around I said to myself 'Keep working' and I did...I didn't let him distract me*

- Ask students to share ideas about how to manage distractions *I put all my stuff away so I don't fiddle with it. I tell myself...don't turn round...keep your eyes and ears on the teacher*

- Alert students to situations where a high level of concentration is needed

- Seat the student close to where the teacher usually stands

- Reduce the distractions within the view of the student such as mobiles, fish tanks etc.

- Keep the student's working area clear of distractions. Allow one small item to 'fiddle' with if this helps the student to focus

- Speak slowly and quietly to bring an impulsive student down to a quieter, more reasonable level. Impulsive students get even more agitated if adults are loud and excitable

- Allow for a cooling off place for an impulsive student who has 'gone over the top'

- Allow some cooling off time for an impulsive student who has 'gone over the top'

- Provide an 'office' (a three sided screen) to place on the student's desk

- Offer the student a separate desk (not as a punishment but a way of helping minimize distractions)

- Provide plenty of opportunities to move around and 'let off steam'

- Structure tasks into short, easy to manage sections

- Give explicit training in seeing one task through to completion without a break

- Use silent reminders. Just move closer to the student and make eye contact

- Encourage the student to self monitor. Give the student a rating card to tick their perception of their own focus at regular intervals

- Break the school day into short sections and give the student positive feedback for periods of positive application

- Older students may need a 'prompter' in important tests or examinations, to make sure they stay on task

- Have fun activities, to practice ignoring distractions. Students are put in pairs and one of each pair has to concentrate on a simple task (such as a dot to dot puzzle). The other partner in the pair has to try to distract the worker in any way that they can, without actually touching them. Obviously roles are reversed, so that each student has a turn of being a 'worker' and a 'distracter'

- Teach the students that 'fast' or 'first' is not necessarily 'best'

- Get students to use the 'pause button', to stop and think before they begin a task

- Distribute work sheets but then ask the students to look at the work sheet for sixty seconds and work out what they have to do before they are allowed to pick up their pencils

- Have fun 'stop and think' activities. Ask the class a series of easy questions which have 'yes' or 'no' answers. The trick is that answers cannot be called out until five seconds has elapsed. Anyone who calls out before that is out, anyone who calls out the wrong answer after five seconds is also out. You can use right hand raised for *Yes* and left hand raised for *No* instead

- Give 'tickets' that entitle students to have a turn speaking in group discussions. Each student has a certain number of tickets, which they need to use economically. Once their tickets are used up they cannot make any more comments. (This is also great for encouraging the less vocal children to take their turn)

- Prepare cards with statements such as *You are working well. You are on task. You stopped and thought. You waited your turn.* Place these cards on the student's desk as appropriate. These cards can be traded off for a small reward

- Introduce relaxation training, yoga, tai chi or any other activity which requires control and quiet reflection

PHYSICAL RESTLESSNESS

Many children and adolescents are restless and fidgety. Sometimes this interferes with their learning and sometimes this does not.

The level of sensory input which each of us needs (children and adults alike) varies considerably. Some people are very comfortable with a low level of sensory input. Children and adults who need a high level of sensory input will always need to be moving, touching, fidgeting to keep their system in its comfort zone of sensory input.

Children with poor muscle tone will also seem restless and fidgety, because they do not have sufficient muscle tone to maintain a steady, controlled position.

Action plans for successful learning

- Arrange appropriate medical assessment and treatment with a paediatrician or occupational therapist if restlessness seriously impacts on the student's learning

- Check to see whether the student's restless, fidgety behaviour actually interferes with their learning. If it does not then no action is needed other than to ensure that other students are not disturbed

- Give the restless student plenty of space so that their restless, fidgety behaviour does not disturb others

- Provide something to 'fiddle' with, such as a squishy ball or a piece of blue tack, for those students who simply 'can't' keep still

- Sitting on the floor is extremely uncomfortable for some students with poor muscle tone. Allow the child to sit on the chair at the edge of the group, rather than on the floor

- Be sure that desk and seat are at an appropriate height/size

- Accept that students with poor muscle tone will have difficulty sitting up straight and will 'slouch' or 'sprawl' as they work

POOR ORGANIZATION

Many dyslexic students often have significant difficulties with organization. Sometimes this is part of their avoidance behaviour, but more often it is a genuine part of their learning disorder.

What is called 'executive function' (looking ahead, planning appropriately, following through etc.) is often a significant problem for the dyslexic student. Dyslexic students often feel overwhelmed because the work is too difficult, or they have too much work to do in the time available. Many dyslexic students have short term memory difficulties or auditory processing problems, and have difficulties writing things down, so they may not have a clear idea about what they are supposed to do.

Dyslexic students often need explicit, clear directions. The poorly organized student often assumes that good organization just 'happens'.

The emotional consequences of dyslexia can also have an impact on personal organization. Students who are depressed or anxious will find it difficult to 'see the big picture' and fail to get themselves well organized.

Action plans for successful learning

- Model good organization so the student can see how it's done

- Brainstorm at home and at school for organization tips that others use

- Set small, achievable goals in aiming to improve organization

- Ask the student to think about organization *How are you going to make sure that you get all of this done by Thursday? How are you going to remember to give this note to your teacher?*

- Ensure the student is equipped with a set of working equipment (pencil, ruler, eraser etc) before the task is started. Have spares readily available to avoid wasting time looking for an essential item

- Get the student to keep all loose papers in one large folder or concertina file

- Get the student a transparent zip wallet. The student decorates it to make it as distinctive as possible (so it is harder to lose!) This then holds all important notices etc that have to be dealt with urgently

- Remind the student to use the wallet. *This is important. Put it in your wallet straight away.*

- At home get the wallet checked *Anything in the wallet today?*

- Negotiate with the student how they want adults to help them *I'd like Mum to write a note and put it on my pillow to remind me to pack my bag*

- Students often rely on adults reminding them over and over again. Teach the student that there will be a limited number of reminders (three is usually plenty) *Last reminder Jess. After this you are on your own with remembering your sports gear*

- Provide structure and routine so that it is easier for good organization to become automatic

- Ask questions rather than give orders. Ask *Today is Tuesday. What do you need to remember?* instead of *It's Tuesday, get your swimming stuff*

- Build 'thinking/planning time' into the schedule at home and at school *OK now stand still for one minute and then tell me what you have to do today*

- Adults should try to avoid constant 'rescue' missions for poorly organized students. For example if sports gear is forgotten, then it stays at home

- Being poorly organized should not mean that the student manages to avoid reasonable, but unwelcome tasks

- Give the student responsibility for organizing pleasant events such as a family outing, a family meal

- Once the responsibility for organizational tasks has been allocated adults should not fuss or interfere

- Clarify 'who does what'. *OK all planned. You are going to take responsibility for everything to do with the drinks, cups, glasses, straws, ice, drinks the whole lot. Here's £10 to buy what you need. I am going to do the sandwiches and Dad is going to do the snacks and nibbles. Drinks are over to you*

- Avoid too many work and play activities to minimize what has to be organized

- Where time limits are relevant, make these explicit to the student and remind the student to use a timer, alarm watch etc to keep track of time

chapter 8

MOTIVATION

WORKLOAD

MOTIVATION, CONFIDENCE AND STRESS

ACCEPTANCE

WORKLOAD

Many dyslexic students have to work extremely hard for very limited results. Frequently the workload flows through to parents, who have to put in a lot of time in supporting the student. Dyslexic students may have the basic class homework, plus unfinished work from school, plus special education homework. Some students will go to extra tutoring or therapy out of school.

> MATHS: In maths am OK but am a bid blow awrich. I stugel in lonirg my tadel I injoy prodlem saveing and reading grichs. My log dvechen iset vere good sort drichen is eser. I have inprooved at every thing and I stagel at But I have stagel much this yare

This student has written MATHS: In maths I am OK but I am a bit below average. I struggle in learning my tables. I enjoy problem solving and reading groups. My long division isn't very good short division is easier. I have improved at everything (that) I struggle at. But I have struggled much this year

If dyslexic students work slowly then they may never finish work in the time available. This is discouraging and sets up poor work habits.

There will be some families spending two or three hours most weekdays in getting their dyslexic primary school student through the set work. Dyslexic students (and their families) can get very tired and discouraged by the seemingly never ending work load.

Work that may have taken hours can look as if it has been rushed through in a few minutes. The combination of high effort and poor outcome is probably one of the most frustrating aspects of dyslexia

> I feel like School is a jail becase The work is to hard and when you do your best they say NOT Good enof

Action plans for successful learning

- Monitor the student in class. Does the student finish the set work in reasonable time if they put in reasonable effort? If not modify the level of difficulty of the work, or the volume of the work required

- Check with parents to see if they feel that their child's work load is manageable or excessive

- Recognize that the dyslexic student may be exhausted by the end of the school day and find extra work really difficult to face

- Make homework consolidation and practice. Keep new or demanding work for the classroom

- Give parents constructive help in supporting the student

  Provide an overview of the week's work ahead of time
  Offer a 'help line' to the parent
  Authorize the parent to abbreviate, modify or support the set work
  Use a home-school communication book for exchange of information about work load

- Set time limits on homework. As a guide

6–7 years of age	Maximum of 15 minutes
7–8 years of age	Maximum of 20 minutes
8–10 years of age	Maximum of 30 minutes
10–12 years of age	Maximum of 45 minutes
12–14 years	Maximum of 75 minutes
14–15 years	Maximum of 90 minutes
16 years plus	Maximum of 180 minutes

- If remedial work is required then reduce the amount of other work set

- If classes are missed to attend remedial sessions or therapy, make time available for catch up work to be done (but do not exclude the student from favourite activities to do this)

- Set short tasks that can be completed in the time available so that the student enjoys a sense of completion and develops good work habits

- Prioritize the work required so that the least important tasks are left until last and omitted if time is short

- If the student falls behind with important pieces of work allow some study time during the school day to catch up (but do not exclude the student from favourite activities to do this)

- Coordinate with other adults so that the student's total workload is integrated and manageable

- Allow the student to take short cuts. There are many suggestions throughout this book of how to do this

- Older students may take fewer subjects to make room for extra study time

- Make sure that the student's day is not 'all work and no play'

MOTIVATION, CONFIDENCE AND STRESS

A dyslexic student often has to go to school, day after day experiencing failure where others are achieving success.

Some dyslexic students become anxious about not being able to cope with requirements. They may fear failure and may limit their efforts in an attempt to avoid failing. Whilst it is important to maintain a student's confidence it is equally important to improve their skill levels so that confidence is on a solid foundation.

Dyslexic students can become very disheartened and depressed by their ongoing difficulties and poor learning outcomes. This may be compounded by the physical and mental fatigue which results from the student's difficulties with learning.

Some students manage to keep a good front at school but are tired, cranky and emotional at home. Most parents give excellent practical and emotional support although some can inadvertently put the dyslexic student under additional pressure.

Action plans for successful learning

- Focus on building up skills as an essential part of building up confidence

- All students are more interested and motivated when they can see the purpose in the task that they are doing

- Always emphasize effort, rather than outcome. A student can always succeed at putting in an effort

- Recognize that motivation comes from expectation of success. Students who expect failure do not feel motivated

- Make praise moderately easy to get. Too easily given praise loses its value

- Keep praise honest, children see through false praise

Adult: *Hey Jack, that's a great GOOD READER badge you've got there*

Jack: *Yeah, all us dumb readers get them*

- Set up learning goals that are realistic

- Make goals explicit so that everyone knows where they are aiming *Cassie will be able to read these five sight words*   not *Cassie will improve her reading*

- Give a time frame for the goal *Cassie will be able to read these five sight words by next Thursday*

- Encourage the student to participate in planning their own, short-term learning goals

- Encourage students to decide what level of challenge they want to go for

  Let's look at the words for next week. See, you are this far along...and this is what we've got left. Now shall we go for the whole six words, or shall we make it three words this week and three words next week?

- Make progress visible by means of record keeping and progress charts

- Encourage the student to mark their own progress on the charts

- Make sure that the student can see that they are learning a lot, and does not feel that they have lots to learn

- Build in frequent tangible rewards (certificates, badges, trophies) for goal achievements

- Provide scope for errors on the way to success

  Felix is aiming to be able to read the 50 most commonly used words

  25 correct: Bronze Award
  40 correct: Silver Award
  50 correct: Gold Award

- Emphasize personal best achievements and celebrate these

- Remember that the advice *Could do better* or *More effort required* is very discouraging if the student really has tried their best

- If a student is a perfectionist who won't take risks set up a paradoxical situation. Show them how to avoid failure by taking a risk

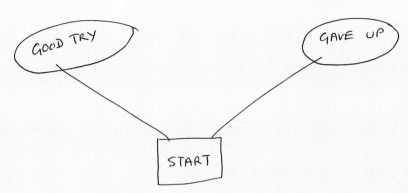

Place counters on the start position. Each time a task is presented the student has to move a counter to GOOD TRY or GAVE UP. If there are more counters on GOOD TRY by the end of the session the student wins. Perfectionists hate to lose!

- Do not make success a burden

Well done, Now you have proved to me that you can do good work I will not accept second best from you in the future Jock

Jock had spent many hours on this piece of work to reach the standard that had pleased his teacher

- Encourage self evaluation *What do you like best in this piece of work? If you were doing it again what would you do differently? Are there any parts where you could have done with some help?*

- Remember that asking for help is often difficult

    The student might think that they are working on the right lines
    The student knows they are in a muddle but does not know the
        right question to ask
    The student may have been reprimanded in the past for asking for help
    The student may feel embarrassed to ask for help

- Encourage and reward problem solving and risk taking. Give stamps, stickers or tickets that can be traded for rewards

You looked for another way to do it
You asked for help
You did not give up
You had kept going until you got it

- Make the praise specific and linked to something which the student has actually done *I'm so proud of you, look how you remembered how to get that 'b' the right way round*

- Avoid giving negatives with positives. Try to keep praise constructive, factual and untainted by negatives *A good idea but spoilt by messy handwriting* is disheartening

- Use multiple grading so that students get feedback for content, effort, neatness, spelling, creativity etc as separate categories so that a poor performance in one category does not wipe out a good performance in another

- Recognize poor motivation as a signal that the student may be feeling depressed

- Seek appropriate medical advice if the student appears to be significantly anxious or depressed

- Make sure the student's program is modified, so that they can see they have a good chance of being successful

- Provide counselling support

- Provide a mentor in school to help the student to negotiate appropriate support

- Ask parents about their view of their child's levels of anxiety or confidence

- Make sure that parents have support and are constructively advised about their role in helping the child

- Deal with parental anxiety by appropriate support for student and family *(see pages 103-105)*

- Give awards for effort and personal best achievements as well as academic and sporting excellence

- Recognize personal qualities such as persistence, fairness, kindness as well as academic and sporting excellence

- Do not insist that the dyslexic student reads out loud in class or writes on the board in front of other students

- Keep test results confidential between student, teacher and parent

- Provide open ended or multi level tasks so that all students can work at their own level without feeling different

- Give alternatives so that students can choose an option that suits them best

ACCEPTANCE

It is, of course, only natural to dislike being seen as different or inferior to others. Although dyslexic students may well need help, they are often reluctant to ask for or to accept it. Intellectually, they may well be equal or brighter than most of their peers, and yet they may feel stupid or dumb. Asking for and accepting help, may confirm this in the student's mind.

Action plans for successful learning

- Where possible, find good role models of older students, or adults who have had dyslexia but have succeeded in spite of this

- Make sure the school classroom environment is a positive one where students respect and support each other

- Provide the student with a card which summarizes their needs. This can be shown to new teachers to clarify what type of support is appropriate

- Create a school climate where receiving help is an accepted part of the learning process

- Be discreet and sensitive about modifying work and giving extra assistance

- Allow the individual dyslexic student to show their talents, so that they are 'different' in a positive way

- Have a clear anti-discrimination and anti-harassment policy within school, where all students know the correct procedures to adopt if discrimination or harassment occurs

- Include the student in all discussions and allow the student to give input and be part of decisions that are made about managing their dyslexia

- Some students have issues with regards to equity *Its not fair that I get more time just because I have dyslexia.* Explain that the intellectual content of the work is what matters and that the time allocation can easily be varied to suit individual needs. *If the test was about how quickly you could write then it would not be fair to give you extra time...but this project is not a speed trial......the project is to test your ideas and understanding so the time you take is not an issue*

- Ensure that the student knows that many hundreds of dyslexic students take senior school and University examinations with the support of special provisions and achieve considerable success

chapter 9

PARENTS, PROFESSIONALS AND HELPERS

PARENTS

ALTERNATIVE OR NEW TREATMENTS FOR DYSLEXIA

PARAPROFESSIONALS AND VOLUNTEERS

PARENTS

Having a dyslexic child can mean additional anxiety and stress for parents. Whilst many parents are concerned about appearing to be fussy and over anxious, they do carry the major responsibility for ensuring that their child has the best opportunities to reach their full potential.

Parents worry about both the practical, and the emotional components of a learning disorder.

From a practical point of view, parents worry about their child falling behind other students of similar age and intelligence. This might mean that the child is not ready to move up to the next year of schooling.

Parents worry that intellectually capable students may fail important subjects because of dyslexic problems in reading, written language, or arithmetic. This could easily result in the student leaving school without qualifications commensurate with their intelligence. Naturally, parents will feel immense anxiety if they can see that this is a possibility.

Parents also worry that their adolescent may not be able to take up further training and education because of dyslexic difficulties. Employment difficulties can also be anticipated. (There are of course many things that can be done to minimize disadvantages such as these, provided the dyslexic student is recognized and given appropriate intervention and adjustments and accommodations. However, parents may not be aware of what can be done.)

Parents may have to meet additional financial costs for assessments, private remedial help, good computer resources etc., to support the dyslexic child. As dyslexia runs in families, some parents may have to meet these financial commitments for several children over many years.

Where there is a family pattern of learning disorder, and ongoing adult dyslexic problems, parents often worry that history is repeating itself in the next generation.

Parents often comment on the fact that their child is distressed and frustrated because of learning difficulties. Many children put a brave face on things at school in front of their peers, but are tired, cranky and distressed at home.

Parents also see their child losing confidence and possibly becoming depressed. This may be a familiar pattern repeating itself from the parent's own childhood. Parents of course also become concerned when the child suffers social consequences because of their learning disorder e.g. being teased, and feeling less happy and confident as a result.

Parents also tell us that the way in which the professionals handle the dyslexic child makes a very important difference.

Parents report major concern when professionals do not seem to have sufficient information about dyslexia to make informed judgments, or when professionals deny that the child has a problem and claim *It will click.* This is a particular problem for families where adult members have enduring and severe learning disorders.

Many parents report anxiety and frustration in situations where professionals do not communicate effectively with one another, so that parents find things which had been agreed on one year are totally unknown to the next year's teacher.

Teachers and parents alike express concern when there is intermittent or inadequate staffing or funding for appropriate remedial programs.

Poor communication between school and home is another source of parental anxiety. Parents may feel that they are not informed about their child's program or progress. This is a particular problem if parents do not understand the jargon or the methods used.

Parents also worry if they believe that inappropriate expectations are being made of the dyslexic child, leading to considerable frustration. For example homework set for the dyslexic child may take many hours to complete. Parents may have to devote a considerable amount of time assisting their dyslexic child. The child may be reluctant and uncooperative.

In the absence of appropriate professional support from school, many parents institute their own home based or private remedial program. The quality and effectiveness of this type of intervention can vary from exceptionally good to disastrous.

Action plans for successful working with parents

- Recognize that it is an essential parental duty to be watchful for the child's interests and to be concerned and act when problems are suspected

- Remember that the concerned parent may have very powerful personal experiences of dyslexia and its impact on their own childhood or adult life

- Acknowledge that the child has a problem and is not lazy

- Avoid giving unsubstantiated reassurance *It will click, he's a boy*

- Arrange for a comprehensive assessment of the child's difficulties

- Set up an appropriate intervention program

- Set up an appropriate classroom support system

- Set up an appropriate classroom learning program

- If resources are not available let the parents know this so that they can explore other options

- Where school resources are limited avoid making judgements about what the parents can afford or will be prepared to do themselves. Let them know the problem and the options and let them make the decision about what to do

- Set achievable goals which are specific and time related *Increase the number of sight words which James can read from thirty words to forty five. This goal will be achieved by October 31st.* This gives parents and student the reassurance of knowing that progress is planned and can be measured unambiguously

- Arrange for regular updates of the student's progress

- Negotiate specific goals with student, parents and professionals so that everyone knows what is happening

- Be particularly aware of the pressure that homework may put on a family. Negotiate with parents and student to keep the homework at a reasonable level

- Use appropriate adjustments and accommodations such as allowing the student to work orally or providing a reader in tests and examinations.

- Modify school tasks and homework, such as shorter tasks, parent scribing for the student etc.

- Demonstrate good teamwork so that parents know there is communication between teachers.

- Foster frequent and honest communication between home and school, so that the parents know what is happening with the student's learning program

- Provide practical support and encouragement so that parents can actively participate in their student's program and have an agreed role in the overall plan

- Maintain good communication between teachers working with the student, particularly between one year and the next

- Make appropriate application for special provisions in public examinations and let the parents know what is being done

ALTERNATIVE OR NEW TREATMENTS FOR DYSLEXIA

It is important that parents and professionals are aware that there are many unscrupulous persons and organizations promoting 'cures' for dyslexia. Over the years, responsible research has continually demonstrated that there are no alternatives, other than quality services provided by appropriately trained, conventional professionals (teachers, speech and language therapists etc.).

All known effective treatments rely on instructional methods, which are based on explicit instruction in the skills of reading and written language or arithmetic. The evidence for the effectiveness of alternative programs which emphasize diet, exercise, or other therapies is very scant indeed.

Parents are, of course, anxious to try any new 'cure' which claims success. It is often very difficult for parents to sort out the charlatans from the genuine professionals, and great caution is often needed.

Action plans for alternative or new 'treatment' programs for dyslexia

- Be very wary of organizations that give themselves grand sounding titles such as 'international', or other titles which on inspection do not relate to any officially recognized international authority or organization

- Ask *Could you give me copies of journal articles relating to this treatment? I am only interested in articles which have been published in reputable journals*

- Be cautious in trusting any promotional material written to look like a genuine scientific document. Unscrupulous operators can sometimes produce a very glossy looking 'scientific article' that is just advertising. If in doubt check with someone who has scientific training such as a doctor or psychologist

- Ask *Could you give me the name of a professional teacher or doctor who could vouch for your treatment?*

- Ask *Would you tell me how you are going to monitor my child's progress?*

- Ask *How will you know when your treatment has been effective?*

- Ask *How will I know if the treatment has been effective?*

- Tell them *I will ask my child's teacher/psychologist/paediatrician to evaluate my child before we start treatment and then after you have finished. Is this acceptable to you?*

- Ask *If your treatment does not work, is there a 'money back guarantee'?*

- Ask *What are your own professional credentials? Could I see copies of the documentation of your qualifications and registration?*

- Ask *I know all professionals have Indemnity Insurance. Could I please see a copy of your Indemnity Insurance?*

- Ask *What are the side effects of your treatment? Could you please show me results of clinical studies, to show that your procedure is absolutely safe?*

- Ask *If we start treatment and I find it is not suiting my child, am I able to stop treatment without further cost to myself?*

- Ask *Can you put me in touch with other people who have used your treatment, who would be able to recommend you?*

- Ask *Could you explain to me what your treatment does, and how it works?*

- Ask *Could you explain to me what the limits of your treatment are? What symptoms or difficulties will it not treat?*

- Tell them *I would like to be able to discuss your proposed treatment with our doctor (or psychologist, teacher etc.). Could you please give me some written information which I can show them*

PARAPROFESSIONALS AND VOLUNTEERS

Paraprofessionals and volunteers are widely used in the support of dyslexic students. Paraprofessionals are generally employed by the school, and have some training but are not fully qualified teachers.

Volunteers may range from highly qualified people such as retired teachers through to unqualified people who are keen to help.

Professionals using the support of paraprofessionals do need to recognize both the advantages and the restrictions involved in the use of paraprofessionals and volunteers in providing services to dyslexic students.

Action plans for working with paraprofessionals and volunteers

- Paraprofessionals must be trained and supervised by appropriate qualified professionals

- Professionals should themselves have appropriate training in the management and utilization of paraprofessionals in the capacity of service providers for dyslexic students

- Ongoing appropriate professional development programs must be made available for paraprofessionals working with dyslexic students

- Paraprofessionals and volunteers should always work under the direct supervision of an appropriately qualified teacher or therapist

- A volunteer or paraprofessional should not be given responsibilities beyond the scope of their expertise

- Volunteers should be used in a supplementary capacity, supporting the efforts of the professionals and paraprofessionals working with a dyslexic student

- At no time, should volunteers be responsible for planning an individual dyslexic student's program, monitoring progress, or reporting to parents or other professionals

- Volunteers do need appropriate training and preparation, before they start to work with any dyslexic student

- Volunteers do need to be accountable to the supervising professional, and good documentation is essential to ensure that all parties know the limits of their responsibilities

- When a paraprofessional is used it is important that the parents know that the student is receiving support from a paraprofessional who is accountable to a fully qualified professional

- When a volunteer is used, it is vital that the parents of the student receiving their services know that the student is receiving support from somebody acting in a voluntary capacity

- Celebrate, nurture and appreciate your volunteers and paraprofessionals. They are an essential part of successful learning for dyslexic students

THE DYSLEXIA CHECKLIST

WORD LIST: THE 100 MOST COMMONLY USED WORDS

GLOSSARY OF PROFESSIONALS

REFERENCES

THE DYSLEXIA CHECKLIST

Glynis Hannell B.Sc (Hons) M.Sc Registered Psychologist

STUDENT DETAILS

Student's Name_____Date_____

Name of person completing checklist_____

Underachievement

- ☐ Difficulties in learning to read, spell or write
- ☐ School work does not reflect their true ability
- ☐ School reports often say 'Could do better'
- ☐ Results do not reflect the effort put in
- ☐ A lot of good teaching input only produces small improvements

Difficulties in combining spoken and written language

- ☐ Slow to learn the link between sounds and letters
- ☐ Can spell a word verbally but cannot write it down
- ☐ Difficulty in getting thoughts on paper
- ☐ Written language has words missing (or extra words)
- ☐ Reads words that are not there
- ☐ Reading lacks fluency and speed

Memory difficulties

☐ Difficulties in remembering instructions

☐ Difficulties in learning basics e.g. letters and their sounds

☐ Problems remembering words from one page to the next

☐ Problems learning sequences e.g. multiplication tables

☐ Can learn spelling for a test but forgets the words very rapidly

☐ Gets the sequence of letters or numbers wrong e.g. 13 for 31, 'on' for 'no'

☐ Difficulties with arithmetic, uses fingers to count

☐ Copies things down incorrectly

☐ Makes the same error over and over again e.g. 'whent'

Speech, phonological and language difficulties

☐ Problems with 'word finding' when speaking

☐ Problems pronouncing long words e.g. 'hostipal'

☐ Problems breaking words into sounds

☐ Difficulties in blending sounds together

☐ Difficulties in recognizing or producing rhymes

☐ Difficulties in learning phonics

☐ Later than average in learning to talk

☐ History of early ear infections

☐ Written language is poorly structured

Visual motor difficulties

- ☐ Slow to learn how to write
- ☐ Poor bookwork, untidy, slow, messy
- ☐ Mixes upper and lower case letters
- ☐ Difficulties in working as fast as other students
- ☐ Poor coordination, clumsy
- ☐ Loses place when reading, uses finger to keep track
- ☐ Letter and number reversals after the age of seven
- ☐ Disliked puzzles and drawing as a younger child
- ☐ Difficulties with sustained writing, hand gets tired very quickly
- ☐ Poor posture, slumps on desk when working, fidgets sitting on the floor

Concentration difficulties

- ☐ Inattentive, in a daydream
- ☐ Easily distracted
- ☐ Diagnosed as having Attention Deficit Disorder
- ☐ Often restless and fidgety
- ☐ Often impulsive, does not stop and think, calls out in class
- ☐ Makes many careless errors
- ☐ Cannot read for more than a short period of time
- ☐ Poor organization, often forgets books, equipment

Social and emotional difficulties

☐   Low self esteem with regards to school work

☐   Avoids learning tasks, 'loses' books, wastes time, 'forgets' homework

☐   Does not expect to succeed so does not try

☐   Gets frustrated and upset when effort does not produce good results

☐   Reluctant to accept help, does not like to be different

☐   Told to 'try harder' even when working very hard

Family history

☐   Other family members have dyslexia or similar learning difficulties

Using the Dyslexia Checklist

Each item that applies to the child or adolescent should be checked off. Even items that only apply occasionally or to a mild degree should be recorded. The more items which apply to a child or adolescent the more likely it is that they are dyslexic. However it is important to remember that several other conditions have similar characteristics and specialist assessment is necessary for formal diagnosis.

WORD LIST: The 100 most commonly used words

These words are the most commonly used words and are the core for good reading and spelling.

Remember that reading always precedes spelling, so never teach a child to spell a word unless they can already read it. You will find ideas for teaching reading and spelling throughout this book.

Set 1

a	in	he	am	the
big	will	come	mum	said

Set 2

it	I	is	go	me
cat	and	dad	look	home

Set 3

like	get	have	can	do
boy	to	see	good	you

Set 4

no	here	girl	all	up
at	that	one	this	she

Set 5

of	was	we	jump	are
play	down	my	live	thing

Set 6

when	new	did	name	yes
run	with	don't	what	little

Set 7

take	put	him	on	some
his	went	into	not	has

Set 8

two	know	can't	her	brother
over	three	sister	them	make

Set 9

away	for	walk	they	way
going	where	give	very	got

Set 10

bring	fall	too	by	let
be	fast	want	only	made

GLOSSARY OF PROFESSIONALS

There are a range of professionals and organisations, who have varying specific expertise, with regards to dyslexia and associated learning disorders. Parents and professionals should be aware of the need for a multi-disciplinary approach to dyslexia. In brief, the following professionals are frequently involved in the management of dyslexia.

Senior members of staff, governors

All dyslexic students need special consideration in their educational programs. The quality of the classroom and special needs support will very much depend on the way in which the school develops and implements its policy regarding students with special needs. The professional support of senior colleagues and management is an essential basis for class teachers and special education teachers to meet the dyslexic students' needs.

Class teachers

The class teacher may often be the first professional to become aware of a student's particular difficulties. They may discuss their concerns with the parents and instigate further assessment. The class teacher's approach will be vital in maintaining the dyslexic student's confidence and motivation.

Class teachers are, of course, responsible for the day to day programming for a student. It is very important that the classroom teacher is aware of the dyslexic student's particular problems and makes appropriate adjustments and accommodations within the classroom. This is not only an appropriate professional response but is, in most countries, a legal requirement, under disability legislation.

Appropriate adjustments, accommodations and teaching strategies have been detailed in other sections of this book. However in brief, the classroom teacher needs to make sure that the student has a fair chance of completing work in a reasonable time frame, and with a reasonable degree of success. This may mean providing supplementary materials such as printed handouts, rather than copying from the board. It may include using modified materials, for example an individualised spelling list. It may involve providing additional support such as a reading buddy.

The classroom teacher will also carry considerable responsibility for supporting the student's self esteem and confidence and monitoring their academic, social and emotional wellbeing.

Specialist teachers

These teachers have particular training and expertise in the management of learning disorders, and are likely to work with a dyslexic student in a one-to-one, or small group situation. They will be responsible for planning and implementing the dyslexic student's remedial program.

Specialist teachers also have expertise in programs, which have been specifically designed for dyslexic students. There are a range of published programs, such as the Orton Gillingham, Hickey and others. Generally speaking, programs for dyslexic students follow a highly structured phonic framework.

Any program (however sound) is only a working tool, at its most effective when used by a skilled teacher who can vary, modify or select what to teach to match an individual student's needs.

The specialist teacher will monitor progress and should be in a position to adjust the student's program as progress is made.

The special education teacher will often liaise with other professionals and with parents to ensure that all the work being done is coordinated and well balanced.

Psychologists

Educational or developmental psychologists are specialists with expertise in assessing children's learning. Their input is essential, in making a differential diagnosis of a student's learning difficulties. The psychological assessment should indicate whether the student does have dyslexia, or has one of the other disorders such as language disorder, general developmental delay, other learning or developmental problems. This is an essential first step, to make sure that the student has dyslexia, and not some other, similar disorder which may need a different type of approach.

Psychologists also provide ongoing support and monitoring. Psychologists can monitor the overall progress of the student, not only from an academic point of view, but also from the point of view of emotional adjustment and coping strategies. Many dyslexic students become anxious, disheartened, or lose motivation. The psychologist will have a role to play in providing counselling and advice to students, parents and teachers.

Psychologists will also be able to provide assessment and advice, with regards to concentration difficulties, including Attention Deficit Disorder. Their input may be required in planning an appropriate management program for an inattentive or impulsive dyslexic student.

Psychologists will also be important in documenting the dyslexic student's learning disorder for the purpose of verifying their eligibility for special programs, special concessionary arrangements for assessment and general legal protection.

Speech and Language Therapists

Speech and Language Therapists (SLTs) have a specialist role to play in the provision of appropriate services for dyslexic students. Speech and language therapists are involved in working on phonological awareness, and other language related skills. Many dyslexic children have some subtle language difficulties, and most have distinct phonological problems.

An SLT will often be an intrinsic part of the overall program for a dyslexic student, working with the phonological and language related skills.

Occupational Therapists

Occupational therapists are likely to be involved with a dyslexic student who has problems with visual motor skills, general coordination, and balance. Dyslexic students who have specific handwriting disorders will often be appropriately seen by an occupational therapist, who will institute a program of treatment for the problems involved in the physical production of written language.

Paediatricians

A paediatrician may be involved in monitoring and supporting a dyslexic child's development. They may be one of the first to recognize a dyslexic disorder emerging in the pre-schooler, or young school child.

A paediatrician is also of vital importance, in diagnosing concurrent problems such as epilepsy and Attention Deficit Disorder. They may also be involved in diagnosis and treatment of emotional or behavioural problems associated with a learning disorder.

Child Psychiatrists

A child psychiatrist will be involved in working with a dyslexic child and adolescent, where emotional or behavioural consequences follow the learning disorder. A psychiatrist can provide ongoing counselling, support and if necessary medication. It may also be the case that the dyslexic student has additional developmental problems, which require the specialist care of a child psychiatrist.

Counsellors

Many schools have student counsellors, and of course there are counsellors in community service and in private practice.

Counsellors can support families and their child or adolescent who has dyslexia. They will provide general advice with regards to parenting, management and coping strategies. They may provide individual counselling for the student with regards to practical coping mechanisms and stress management.

Support Organizations

In most developed countries there are support organizations for dyslexics, their families and professionals who work with dyslexics. These organizations may organize conferences, publish professional journals, facilitate information exchange, run a special interest library, resource collection or book shop. Some may run training programs and offer accreditation to teachers or schools that meet acceptable standards. Some organizations run a referral service to help parents or adult dyslexics find reputable service providers.

Legal Services

Dyslexia is a recognized disability in most developed countries. In situations where discrimination occurs and cannot be resolved at 'grassroots' level, legal advice may be needed to pursue redress through legal channels.

REFERENCES

Abidin, R.R. (1995) *Parenting Stress Index (3rd edn)* Odessa, FL: Psychological Assessment Resources

Adams, M.J. (1990) Word Recognition: The interface of educational policies and scientific research. *Reading and Writing: An Interdisciplinary Journal,* 5, 113–139

American Psychiatric Association (1994) *Diagnostic and statistical manual of mental disorders (4th edn).*Washington, DC

Block, C.C., Pressley, M. (2002) *Comprehension Instruction: Research based best practices.* New York: Guilford Press

Broomfield, H., Combley, M. (1997) *Overcoming Dyslexia: A practical handbook for the classroom.* London: Whurr Publishers

Brown, G.D.A., Ellis, N.C. (Eds) (1994) *Handbook of Spelling: Theory, process and intervention.* Chichester: Wiley

Dyson, L.L. (1996) The experiences of families of children with learning disabilities: parental stress, family functioning, and sibling self-concept. *Journal of Learning Disabilities,* 29, 280–286

Elbro, C., Borstrom, I., Peterson, D.K. (1998) Predicting dyslexia from Kindergarten: The importance of distinctness of phonological representations of lexical items. *Reading Research Quarterly,* 33, 36–60

Felton, R.H. (1933) Effects of instruction on the decoding skills of children with phonological processing problems. *Journal of Learning Disabilities,* 26(9), 583–589

Fisher, P. (1999) Getting up to speed. *Perspectives,* 25(2),12–13

Foorman, B.R., Francis, D.J., Winidates, D. *et al.* (1997) Early interventions for children with reading disabilities. *Scientific Studies in Reading,* 1, 255–276

Foorman, B.R., Francis, D.J., Fletcher, J.M., *et al.* (1998) The role of instruction in learning to read: Preventing reading failure in at risk children. *Journal of Educational Psychology,* 90, 37–55

Fuller, G.B., Rankin, R.E. (1994) Differences in levels of parental stress among mothers of learning disabled, emotionally impaired, and regular school children. *Perceptual and Motor Skills*, 78, 583–592

Graham, S.,Voth,V.P. (1990) Spelling instruction: Making modifications for students with learning disabilities. *Academic Therapy*, 4, 447–457

Grigorenko, E.L. (2001) Developmental dyslexia: An update and genes, brains and environments. *Journal of Child Psychology and Psychiatry*, 42, 91–125

Henry, M.K. (1997) The decoding/spelling continuum. *Dyslexia: An International Journal of Research and Practice*, 3(3), 178–189

Latson, S.R. (1987) Preventing parent burnout: Model for teaching effective coping strategies to parents of children with learning disabilities. Reprinted in *Learning Disabilities Association, LDA Newsbriefs Jan/Feb* 1995 (reprinted from the 1987 issues of LDA Newsbriefs)

Lovett, M., Borden, S., DeLuca, T., Lacerenza, L., Benson, N. & Brackstone (1995) Treating the core deficits of developmental dyslexia: evidence of transfer of learning following strategy and phonologically based reading training programs. *Developmental Psychology*, 3: 805–822

Lyon, G.R. (Ed.) (1994) *Frames of reference for the assessment of learning disabilities.* Baltimore, MD: Brookes Publishing

MacArthur, C.A. (1996) Using technology to enhance the writing processes of students with learning disabilities. *Journal of Learning Disabilities*, 29: 344–354

McArthur, G.M.and Bishop, D.V.M. (2001) Auditory perceptual processing in people with reading and oral language impairments: Current issues and recommendations. *Dyslexia*, 7, 150–170

Morrison, G.M.and Cosden, M.A. (1997) Risk, resilience, and adjustment of individuals with learning disabilities. *Learning Disability Quarterly*, 20, 43–60

Muter, V., Snowling, M., (1997) Grammar and phonology predict spelling in middle childhood. *Reading and Writing*, 9, 407–425

National Reading Panel (2000) *Teaching Children to Read: An evidence-based assessment of the scientific research literature on reading and its implications for reading instruction.* Washington DC: National Institute of Child Health and Human Development

Oakland, T., Black, J.L., Stanford, G., Nussbaum, N.L. and Balise, R. (1998) An evaluation of the dyslexia training program: A multisensory method for promoting reading in students with reading disabilities. *Journal of learning Disabilities*, 31, 140–147

Pinnell, G.S., De Ford, D. and Lyons, C. (1988) *Reading Recovery: Early intervention for at risk first graders.* Arlington, VA: Educational Research Service

Rasinski, T. (1990) Effects of repeated reading and listening while reading on reading fluency.*Journal of Educational Research*, 83, 147–150

Rayner, K., Foorman, B.R., Perfetti, C.A. *et al.* (2002) How should reading be taught? *Scientific American*, 286 (3), 85-91

Resta, S.P. and Eliot, J. (1994) Written expression in boys with attention deficit disorder. *Perceptual and Motor Skills*, 79(3), 1131–1138

Rowe, K.J. and Rowe, K.S. (1992) The relationship between inattentiveness in the classroom and reading achievement. *Journal of the American Academy of Child and Adolescent Psychiatry*, 31(2), 349–368

Sattler, J.M. (1992) *Assessment of children* (3rd edn, revised and updated). San Diego, CA: Jerome M. Sattler

Semrud-Clikeman, M., Biederman, J., Sprich-Buckminster, S. *et al.* (1992) Comorbidity between ADHD and learning disability. *Journal of the American Academy of Child and Adolescent Psychiatry*, 31, 439–448

Snowling, M. (1995) Phonological processing and developmental dyslexia. *Journal of Research in Reading*, 18(2), 132–138

Snowling, M. and Hulme, C. (1997) *Dyslexia biology cognition and intervention.* London: Whurr Publishers

Snowling, M. (2000) *Dyslexia (2nd edn).* Oxford: Blackwell

Snowling, M. Bishop, D.V.M. and Stothard, S.E.(2000) Is preschool language impairment a risk factor for dyslexia in adolescence? *Journal of Child Psychology and Psychiatry*, 41, 587–600

Sparrow, S.S., Balla, D.A. and Cicchetti, D.V. (2000) *Comprehensive psychological and psychoeducational assessment of children and adolescents: A developmental approach.* Boston, MA : Allyn & Bacon

Stackhouse, J. (2000) Barriers to literacy development in children with speech and language difficulties. In D.V.M. Bishop, L.B. Leonard (Eds) *Speech and Language Impairments in Children: Causes, characteristics and outcomes.* Philadelphia Psychology Press Ltd

Torgensen, J.K., Wagner, R.K. and Raschotte, C.A. (1997) Prevention and remediation of severe reading disabilities: Keeping the end in mind. *Scientific Studies in Reading,* 1(3), 2117–2134

Turner, M. (1997) *The psychological assessment of dyslexia.* London: Whurr Publishers

World Health Organisation (2000) *ICIDH-2: International classification of functioning, disability and health.* Geneva.

Wolf, M. and Bowers, P. (1999) The question of naming speed deficits in developmental reading disabilities: An introduction to the double deficit hypothesis. *Journal of Educational Psychology,* 91, 1–24

Wright, B.A., Bowen, R.W. and Zecker, S.G. (2000) Nonlinguistic perceptual deficits associated with reading and language disorders. *Current Opinions in Neurobiology,* 10, 482–486